Contemporary
African American
Preaching

Also by L. Susan Bond:
Trouble with Jesus: Women, Christology, and Preaching

Contemporary African American Preaching

Diversity in Theory and Style

L. Susan Bond

CHALICE
PRESS

ST. LOUIS, MISSOURI

Cover art and design: Elaine Young
Interior design: Hui-chu Wang
Art direction: Michael Domínguez

This book is printed on acid-free, recycled paper.

Visit Chalice Press on the World Wide Web at
www.chalicepress.com

10 9 8 7 6 5 4 3 2 1   03 04 05 06 07 08

Library of Congress Cataloging–in–Publication Data

Bond, L. Susan.
  Contemporary African American preaching / L. Susan Bond.
     p. cm.
  Includes bibliographical references.
  ISBN 0-8272-0489-2 (alk. paper)
  1. African American preaching. I. Title.
  BV4208.U6 B66 2002
  251'.0089'96073–dc21

                                                    20020077

Printed in the United States of America

This volume is dedicated
to my brothers in the faith,
Rufus Burrow, Jr., and Lewis V. Baldwin, Jr.,
mentors and tormentors
who taught me to know and to love
the other half of my faith tradition.

Contents

Acknowledgments

I want to offer recognition and gratitude to the following people, without whom this audacious project would have been nearly unthinkable.

To the late Sam Proctor and the vivid Gardner Taylor, who offered the kind of premature and gracious encouragement that was necessary to begin such an audacious project. I am humbled by your support.

To Wallace Charles Smith, Pastor of Shiloh Baptist Church, Washington, D. C., and former prof, who taught me to love the evangelical tradition of Black Homiletics, who prayed with me and reminded me of our common racial inheritance through Native Americans.

To my dear colleagues, Rufus Burrow, Jr., an African American ethicist, and Lewis V. Baldwin, Jr., an African American historian, whose trust in my abilities never wavered. I give thanks for their diligence in tutoring me this far, and for their willingness to be mentors and tormentors. I cannot begin to say thanks enough.

To David Buttrick, who is always a serious student of the African American homiletic tradition and who taught me to love homiletic theory. For all your grace, David, much thanks.

To Martha J. Simmons, sister-homiletician, who believed in this project and offered practical insights into getting materials. For late night talks and scrupulous e-mails, thank you.

To Joe Webb, smart homiletician, excellent friend and colleague, who read parts of the manuscript and offered excellent advice. Thanks for the phone calls, e-mails, and editorial savvy.

To Jon L. Berquist, editor, confidante, and dear friend, who never quit believing that I would bring this project to fruition. For years of faithfulness, much thanks.

To my colleague and fellow Hombrat, Bob Howard, bibliographer and research librarian par excellence, who contributed most of the bibliographic material. The Vandy Library will miss you sorely.

To Nancy Weatherwax, a dogged research assistant, who tracked down womanist literature. Thank you, Nancy, for all your good work.

To Laura "Sissie" Prigmore, who offered bribes and rewards for pages completed and who kept raising the bar at every opportunity. Thank you, counselor and sistah, for requiring ongoing accountability.

To J. Coffey May, my man-child. And to his sister, Megan May, whose joy for life intoxicates. Thank you for loving your academic mama and for cheering the completion of each chapter.

Preface

The African American Christian tradition has produced a lion's share of America's great preachers. In fact, many Americans consider the African American pulpit the pinnacle of religious oratory. We can all name a few famous African American preachers, and some can call an even more impressive roll. During February's Black History Month, we are reminded of Martin Luther King, Jr.'s astonishing homiletical gifts, and for the rest of the year we can channel-surf the television to catch E. L. Franklin, Jeremiah Wright, Charles Adams, or T. D. Jakes. Novice preachers of all races study the pacing, delivery, and phraseology of the pulpit giants. If you want to learn from the best preachers, you might well focus on African American preachers.

This is an introductory work on contemporary homiletic theory among African American academic homileticians. *The purpose of this work is to demonstrate the variety of preaching theories and styles that actually characterize African American preaching at the close of the twentieth century.* While parish ministers and theological students are apt to speak of "a black style" or "black preaching" as if it were monolithic, such a situation is hardly the case. This book will survey the "gentlemen preachers" of an older rhetorical style; afrocentrists who argue for a particular cultural and racial difference; celebrationists who favor a cathartic structure; liberation or social crisis preachers committed to social activism; a growing number of pastoral care theorists; and an emerging group of womanist and black feminist homileticians.[1] Certainly to take the tradition of African American preaching with due seriousness is to take account of the real diversity within it, and to avoid leveling it to a static phenomenon. My own earlier work with women's theologies for preaching is driven by a similar concern to acknowledge real difference within communities of discourse that are frequently treated as if they were without nuance or conflict.[2]

---

[1]Afrocentrism, or Africentrism, is discussed in a later section, and more thoroughly in the chapter on Henry Mitchell. J. Deotis Roberts has recently written extensively about Africentric Christianity and surveys the range of options, including a good discussion of Molefi Kete Asante's work. See J. Deotis Roberts, *Africentric Christianity: A Theological Appraisal for Ministry* (Valley Forge, Pa.: Judson Press, 2000).

[2]L. Susan Bond, *Trouble With Jesus: Women, Christology and Preaching* (St. Louis: Chalice Press, 1999).

To date, the most recent books on African American homiletic theory have either promoted a particular theological approach, a particular method, or a broad-based historical apologetic for African American preaching. Almost nothing has been written within the last thirty years that deals critically with similarities and differences within the field itself. Charles V. Hamilton wrote *The Black Preacher in America* in 1972, a historical overview that set the phenomenon of African American preaching against the backdrop of social and political changes within American history. Lawrence L. Beale wrote *Toward a Black Homiletic* in 1978, but this was a focused look at a constructive homiletic based on two African American homileticians. Henry M. Mitchell has written extensively on African American homiletics, but he argues for a "black style" and tends to minimize differences between theorists, setting African American preaching against the Eurocentric theories he rejects. Mervyn Warren's *Black Preaching: Truth and Soul,* 1977, explored contemporary sermons for rhetorical style and effect. Warren's work recognized broad rhetorical diversity and attempted a typology of African American styles. Evans Crawford and James Harris have recently written particular theories and methods, including brief overviews of "the black tradition." Crawford's work (*The Hum: Call and Response in African American Preaching,* 1995), however, is greatly influenced by ritual theory, while Harris (*Preaching Liberation,* 1995) is arguing (à la James H. Cone) for an African American liberation theology. There is little within the last two decades that offers an analytical survey of contemporary African American homileticians. Moreover, there is nothing to date that surveys the contributions of African American women and womanists to homiletic theory and sets their scholarship in conversation with other African American theorists and/or EuroAmerican homiletic theory.

My interest in African American preaching began more than ten years ago as an attempt to become more familiar with the diversity in American cultural forms of religious expression. My first book, *Trouble with Jesus: Women, Christology, and Preaching,* explores a different population, but with the same attention to issues of theology, homiletic theory, and diverse cultural expressions. That work was far more evaluative and constructive than this one, a liberty I took by virtue of being part of the women's homiletic tradition.

In this project, it is my desire to be descriptive and analytical, without offering a constructive argument. I do not pretend to know the African American preaching tradition from the inside. I am a white, middle-class academic, studying the tradition from a situation of cultural distance. I hope to do so with respect, reasonable knowledge, and a certain familiarity. Theo Witvliet is a white Dutch academic, author of *The Way of the Black Messiah,* who offers criteria for white scholars writing about aspects of African American religion, including a genuine familiarity with written scholarship, a respect for the scholarship, and a critical stance informed primarily by scholars inside the tradition under consideration.[3] I do not presume to speak on behalf of African American churches or preachers. I work as an outsider, attempting to understand a tradition that is both dear and somewhat removed from me. As African American scholars have claimed, and as Mary Douglas, social anthropologist, has written, there is a certain epistemological advantage to being an outsider. I write, self-consciously, as an outsider.

---

[3]Theo Witvliet, *The Way of the Black Messiah: The Hermeneutical Challenge of Black Theology as a Theology of Liberation,* trans. John Bowden (London, England: SCM Press LTD, 1987), 4–10.

Introduction

There is a popular assumption that the black preaching tradition is distinct and identifiable. What is interesting for the student of homiletics is that while many argue for a defined set of African American homiletic characteristics, there is little agreement on what these characteristics are.[1]

When people try to characterize what makes African American preaching distinctive, they frequently attend to matters of style and delivery. A young preacher or student of preaching might well locate some articles that offer insights into the genius of African American preaching and would be introduced to issues that include matters of style and delivery but that also go beyond those dimensions into theological and hermeneutical issues. The trend in recent decades has been to identify what is characteristic about the form and content of African American sermons themselves, not just the delivery of them. Some have characterized African American preaching as distinctively narrative in form, distinctively climactic, moving toward a narrative as well as an oratorical celebration. Others have attended to particular

---

[1]See Olin Moyd's article "Elements in Black Preaching," *Journal of Religious Thought*, 30/1 (Spring/Summer 1973): 52–62; James Henry Harris, "Preaching Liberation: The Afro-American Sermon and the Quest for Social Change," *Journal of Religious Thought* 46/2 (1989–90): 7ff; Leontine T. C. Kelly, "Preaching in the Black Tradition," in *Women Ministers,* ed. Judith L. Weidman (San Francisco: Harper & Row, 1985), 67–76; Lyndrey A. Niles, "Rhetorical Characteristics of Traditional Black Preaching," *Journal of Black Studies* 15 (1984): 41–52.

1

theological themes and commitments, particularly to theological issues of liberation and social justice.

Olin Moyd has claimed that distinctively African American preaching is characterized by narrative and repetition, while the structure attends to testimony, liberation, and celebration. James Harris claims that christology is primary among African American preachers and that Jesus as Liberator is the characteristic of genuine "Afrocentric" preaching. This happens when preaching is "Prototypically Black," proud of African heritage, socially critical, liberative, and celebrative. Leontine Kelly claims that Black Preaching is narrative and affirming. Lyndrey Niles draws almost entirely on Henry Mitchell (*Black Preaching*, Philadelphia: J.B. Lippincott, 1970) for the categories of sermon structure, which include introduction (personal identification with preacher), imaginative retelling of the Bible story, and a celebrative climax. He follows Mitchell in terms of style characteristics, claiming that Black Preaching has linguistic flexibility (well-turned phrase, Black English), cadence, call, and response. We'll discuss the emergence of self-consciously "Black Preaching" in a later section.

What's pertinent at this point is that the categories overlap, but not with enough uniformity to claim that black preaching is significantly different from passionate narrative sermons from white Baptist pulpits. We could just as easily argue that African American preaching is simply representative of Baptist preaching styles. What is frequently overlooked, however, are the implicit homiletical theories and theologies that underlie preaching method and sermon preparation. Every preacher has some implied assumptions about why preachers preach, what preachers are supposed to preach about, what preaching is supposed to accomplish, and how to craft a sermon that will meet all these expectations.

Cleophus LaRue has recently written what may be the most careful articulation of the distinctiveness of African American preaching, identifying a particular hermeneutic approach to the Bible, a particular understanding of God's providence, and a set of homiletical "domains" or contemporary concerns that clearly distinguish African American preaching.[2] He traces these elements through a careful examination of nineteenth- and twentieth-century preachers and their sermons. He is to be congratulated for going beyond stylistic concerns and into the heart

---

[2]Cleophus LaRue, *The Heart of Black Preaching* (Louisville: Westminster John Knox Press, 2000).

of theological themes. LaRue's consideration of biblical hermeneutics and theological issues may in fact set the context for the concerns of this current project. Where previous writers have offered somewhat reductionistic "theological themes," LaRue's work actually opens the door for considering diversity within some general contours. However, it is only by expanding the categories in such a way that LaRue can argue convincingly for some common homiletical ground.

This book proposes to explore the unexamined diversity within African American homiletical theories. Attending to those who have been prominent teachers of preachers may provide a critical, if unusual, starting point. Rather than focusing on popular preachers, we will attend to the academic discipline of homiletics and to homiletic theory in particular. Some readers will take exception to the idea that we can learn anything about a tradition from its theorists. At almost every point in this project, we can well imagine particular preachers who are exceptions to these claims. Vernon Johns, the immediate predecessor of Martin Luther King, Jr., at Dexter Avenue Baptist Church, King himself, and a variety of other "unsung" homiletical heroes will come to mind. Others have chronicled the works and ideas of popular preachers, and it is only my intention to shift the gaze from popular preachers to homiletic theorists that creates a conflict. This project is intentionally limited to homiletic theoreticians and does not attend to the quite public work of particular popular preachers.

We survey several of the most well-known homiletical theorists to identify not the similarities, but the differences between homiletic theories. Exploring the similarities would only flatten out the fullness of any particular theory in an attempt to develop an overarching "unified theory" of African American preaching. To give each homiletician his or her due requires us to carefully articulate how their different theological perspectives produce different methods of sermon preparation and delivery, different strategies for selecting illustrative material, even different ways of beginning and ending sermons. To demystify the notion of a monolithic tradition is not disrespectful, nor does it undercut LaRue's observations, but is fully respectful of the richness and nuance contained within a powerful cultural expression.

1

African American Preaching and Homiletic Theory

While no one has actually clearly defined the specifics of that turf we call homiletic theory, some common divisions seem apparent. Homiletic theory generally deals with theological and methodological issues in preaching and the connection between theology and method. If, for example, a preacher assumes that the purpose of preaching is to teach doctrinal truths, the homiletical form and delivery will follow that task as the preacher takes a certain doctrine as a topic, explores it in an occasionally didactic manner, and rationally argues for its acceptance. If, on the other hand, preaching is geared to produce guilt and subsequent conversion/confession, we could expect a sermon form that focuses early on convicting the sinners of their guilt and rises to a call for repentance. Preaching that intends to comfort the afflicted will be more soothing and pastoral than prophetic preaching that intends to afflict the comfortable. Or if the homiletical task is to teach biblical literacy, one might expect long expository sermons full of ancient cultural detail and a subsequent application to contemporary life.

Homiletic theory, or the integration of theology and method, is at the heart of every sermon, whether we recognize it or not. To make our work manageable, we will consider each major homiletical theory relative to some identifiable categories. These categories will include theological assumptions about the nature of the gospel, the purpose of preaching, the relationship between preaching and scripture, the relationship between testaments, the nature and purpose of faith communities, the relationship between preaching and liturgy, the relationship of preaching to African American studies, the relationship of preaching to language theories, and the relationship to other contemporary theological issues (narrative theologies, postliberalism, existentialism, liberation theologies, etc.).

The analytical categories proposed and discussed do not in any way represent a disciplinary consensus within the white homiletic tradition or the African American homiletic tradition. As with all attempts at typological schemes, the one proposed here will strike some as incomplete or inappropriate. As a white scholar attempting conversation between the two contextual traditions, I am suggesting these categories as the most fruitful for internal analysis and for analysis across and between different traditions. The categories have been hinted at, suggested, by a somewhat inductive method of extensive reading within both homiletic traditions to see what interests and topics seem to emerge with regularity. In part, I have proposed these categories as a way of generating discussion rather than limiting the range of discourse, and of extending the conversation to include the interests of African American women theologians and womanist homiletical works. My own academic interest in systematic and constructive theology is certainly apparent in this survey, indicating my own assumption that preaching is a thoroughly theological activity (or theoethical, as Katie Cannon would claim) demanding careful thought, along with in-house (confessional) and public (apologetic) claims.[1]

In this last regard, such attempts to "type" homiletic theologies for public conversation seem to be respectful of African American homiletics itself, as an endeavor to make public the faith claims of particular communities. Such an approach takes seriously the most deeply held claims of believers and their spokespersons to demonstrate in particular ways how Christian faith takes shape with regard to particular self-understandings and particular social locations within public life.

---

[1] I use the term *apologetic* to refer to the traditional theological category of making a public argument, not in the sense of expressing remorse or sorrow.

Nature of the Gospel

At the very least, preachers understand their own preaching to be in some relationship to the proclamation of Jesus and the early church in announcing the good news. The gospel, or the good news, however, is an empty category unless we articulate exactly what the good news is and for whom it is glad tidings. A group of theological students will readily agree to the proposition that the church should preach the gospel, but they will likely fall into an uneasy silence if you ask precisely what the good news is.

For some the gospel is good news about personal salvation from the consequences of sin; for others the gospel is the good news that Jesus offers sociopolitical liberation within history. Gospel articulations usually involve some combination of christology (the person of Jesus), soteriology (the particulars of salvation), and anthropology (sin and the human situation). Obviously, given the variety of possibilities within christology, soteriology, and anthropology, any combination of the three into a theology of proclamation will produce a number of different approaches. What constitutes sin? What are its consequences? What constitutes salvation, and what are its consequences? How does the transformation between sin and salvation occur? Jesus may be a sacrificial lamb offered as a substitute to a righteously indignant deity, or Jesus may be a victim of human sin, a prototype of the oppressed minority. Our salvation may be an after-death reprieve from the terrors of hell, an inner tranquility that allows us to find the present meaningful, or a real liberation from literal captivity.

Homileticians not only vary from one another in their particular formulations but occasionally demonstrate a noticeable inconsistency within their own approaches. Sometimes the internal inconsistencies can be attributed to variations within a continuum. For example, a homiletician might make claims about the gospel or good news in recognition of the possibility that salvation is a matter of spiritual and social liberation, and will make both rhetorical arguments within a discussion or a sermon. In this case, the homiletician acknowledges a variety of approaches and employs a variety himself or herself. However, some homileticians do not acknowledge variety; they are just plain contradictory. An example of this would be a homiletician who claims that God is unconditionally loving and forgiving, while actually making counterarguments that nonbelievers will perish in damnation. Internal contradictions within homiletic theologies and theories are frequently glossed over by an appeal to "mystery" or "paradox."

Every homiletic theory has some implicit theology of the good news within its foundational assumptions, and understandings of the good news have an impact on what theoreticians propose as the homiletical task. The assumptions about the nature of the gospel almost always result in particular methodological preferences expressed in sermon design. We will explore assumptions about the nature of the gospel to trace out the implications for any particular theoretical and methodological approach.

Purpose of Preaching

Closely related to the nature of the gospel is the purpose of preaching. One of the ways to approach the issue is to ask the question, "What would happen if we did not preach?" If the gospel is related to a content, it is also related to a rhetorical intention. We preach x for y to happen. Regardless of the particulars of the good news, homileticians also make assumptions about what this proclamation is supposed to produce in the hearers. However, it is just as likely that preachers do not give sustained or explicit attention to this question. If pressed, we can usually offer some answer, but it's the rare preacher who has given the notion critical attention. We preach because…well…that's what we do.

Homiletical purposes come in a variety of forms. We preach so that souls will be saved, so that hearts will be changed, so that behaviors will improve, so that social structures will be challenged, so that congregations will be instructed, so that communities will be formed, and so on. We preach the good news toward some anticipated outcome, and that anticipated outcome likewise implies certain methodological and design preferences. If we assume that the purpose of preaching is to move individuals to repentance, we likely will preach sermons that open with indictment and close with invitation. If we assume that the purpose of preaching is to impart information, our sermons will be developed like outlines or lesson plans, with summaries of points at the end and with mnemonic devices for remembering the main ideas (humility, harmony, honesty, and heroism). If preaching is primarily for moral instruction, we can expect to find moralistic sermon illustrations, such as what happens to the unsaved and what benefits there are for the righteous. Obviously there are combinations of these implied purposes, but usually one dominant purpose rises to the surface of a homiletic theory to suggest methodological and design preferences.

Within twentieth-century homiletic theory (African American and white) a popular assumption was that the dominant purpose of preaching is to move individual hearers to some kind of inner experience. Since most American homiletic theory of the last two centuries bore the imprint of revivalism in a variety of forms, we are not terribly surprised. A slightly different version of revival piety emerged in the middle of the twentieth century with the popularity of existential philosophy and psychology, suggesting that a new self-understanding was the primary purpose of preaching the good news. In general, revival or therapeutic approaches blunt prophetic dimensions of the gospel and overlook the possibilities of communal vocation.

Relationship between Preaching and Scripture

One of the most explicit assumptions within contemporary homiletic theory is that the content of preaching is a scriptural passage and that one of the primary purposes of preaching is to make the scriptures available for public reflection. It is probably fair to say that within contemporary American homiletic theory (whether African American or white), a high doctrine of scripture operates as the key to homiletical reflection. How this relationship is integrated into the nature of the gospel and the purpose of preaching makes homiletic theory even more complex. What happens in most homiletic theory is that the content of preaching shifts from proclamation of the gospel to the explication of a text, and usually for the purpose of creating some inner experience for individual believers. This confusion about homiletic content tends to confuse homiletic purpose. If we believe that the good news is compelling for moving hearers to some experience, why, then, preach from the Bible?

This confusion probably stems from two understandings of the phrase "Word of God." Some homileticians assume, along with Karl Barth, that the written word of God is the sole content of proclamation and that the gospel is what we distill from that scriptural witness. Barth argued that preaching was to be an exposition of scripture and that preachers were not supposed to talk *about* scripture or *about* the ideas in it, but talk *from* scripture. "There is no place at all for the *scopus* of a sermon, whether theoretical (a formal theme or impressive proposition) or practical (the aim of directing listeners to a certain type of conduct)...If they offer their congregation a clever conceptual picture, even though it be arrived at by serious and intensive exegesis, it will not be scripture itself that speaks, but something will merely be said *about* scripture."[2] Since revelation has occurred and has ended, we are in a different position, Barth claims, than the early writers and apostles. We may not rely on our interpretations, on big ideas, or on any concern for systematic theology, but only on the text itself. "The sermon will be like the involuntary lip movement of the one who is reading with great care, attention, and surprise, more following the letters than reading in the usual sense, all eyes, totally claimed, aware that 'I have not written the text.'"[3]

Barth's claims will come as a surprise to many homileticians and preachers who are tempted to extrapolate a Barthian homiletic from Barth's more popular and famous admonition to preach with the Bible in one hand and the newspaper in the other.[4] The later Barth eschews any attempts at relevance, originality, existential philosophy, sermon introductions, and even illustrations! He writes that he regrets his earlier attempts to make preaching relevant or contextual, and wishes he had not once preached about the war. "Preachers should be good marksmen who aim their guns beyond the hill of relevance."[5]

The Reformers, however (particularly Luther and Calvin), tended to suggest that the *spoken* word of good news proclamation was the "Word of God" to which the biblical record testified. What we notice is that there are two paradigms, each a reverse of the other, for the relationship between the written scriptures and the proclamation of the gospel. For the early church, the content of preaching was the good news about Jesus the Christ, his ministry, crucifixion, and resurrection. The earliest Christians did not have the New Testament to preach from. Later, in the last two centuries, as the doctrine of biblical inspiration became more rigid, the pattern reversed. Bible verses became the content of preaching, leaving open the possibility that one could preach from the Bible without ever preaching the saving glad tidings of God's amazing grace. The Word as a proclamation of grace and the Word as a written

---

[2]Karl Barth, *Homiletics* (Louisville: Westminster John Knox Press, 1991, reprint of 1966 German edition), 49. The term *scopus* is analogous to a theme or topic.

[3]Ibid., 76.

[4]Karl Barth, *The Epistle to the Romans* (New York: Oxford University Press, 1968, trans. 1933 original), 425. It is not clear that Barth was recommending a wide reading of contemporary secular literature–especially of newspapers!–for the purposes of relevance. One *could* interpret his comments the opposite way, in fact, as a rejection of "abstracting from context."

[5]Barth, *Homiletics,* 119.

document reversed positions, with the written document serving as the gatekeeper of homiletics. We have only recently lost the idea that the gospel can be preached with or without the Bible and that the scripture is the handmaiden of the good news, not the mother of it. We will explore the position that each homiletician accords to the written canon and the relationship between the scriptures and preaching. Must preaching always be biblical? Must preaching be subject to exegetical rules or theological rules? How are differences adjudicated? If a text is sexist, do we preach it? What grants authority to proclamation if we don't have a high doctrine of scripture?[6]

Cleophus LaRue's work on African American preaching tackles this same issue when he argues that one of the distinctive marks of that tradition is its particular hermeneutic approach to the biblical texts. He first notes the centrality of the Bible to preaching, and then suggests a particular pattern of interpretation in which the preacher seeks "a sovereign God who acts in concrete and practical ways on behalf of the marginalized and powerless…this foundational biblical hermeneutic provides us with a means for understanding the sense in which exposition of scripture and the life situations of blacks come together consistently and creatively in black preaching."[7]

The Relationship between Testaments

As soon as you claim a biblical authority, you are confronted with the problem of which biblical authority is really authoritative. And here's where the understanding of the nature of the gospel comes back into play. If the gospel is good news because it reverses some previous theological "misunderstanding," then part of the preaching task is to clearly delineate the uniqueness of Jesus and the special nature of the gospel. On the other hand, if the gospel is good news that is consistent with Jewish monotheism, then the homiletical task is to demonstrate the continuity of God's purposes throughout. These two options are contradictory. God cannot be doing both a radically new thing and an old thing at the same time. How we make sense of this derives from our christological claims about the nature of God in Jesus the Christ. Was God doing something radically new and different in Jesus the

---

[6]See an interesting article by Ed Farley, "Preaching the Bible and Preaching the Gospel," *Theology Today*, April 1994.

[7]Cleophus LaRue, *The Heart of Black Preaching* (Louisville: Westminster John Knox Press, 2000), 18–19.

Christ? Or was God using Jesus to renew our understanding of the same promises and providence to which the First Testament witnesses?

J. Alfred Smith, pastor of Allen Temple Baptist Church, has taught homiletics and Christian ministry at the American Baptist Seminary of the West, at the Graduate Theological Union of Berkeley, California, and at Fuller Theological Seminary. He has written extensively about homiletics and particularly about Christian preaching from the Hebrew Bible. Smith has identified common theological problems that surface in preaching with regard to the relationship between the testaments, problems that surface homiletically as a prejudice against Jews and Israel.

> Some persons have decided that since the coming of Jesus and the establishing of the New Testament, the only function of the Old Testament is historical. This idea is supported by the anti-Pharisee bias that views the Pharisees as biblical antichrists. The Pharisees are seen as persons who rejected Jesus and embraced Old Testament Law. The bias against the Pharisees has influenced certain persons not only to discard the Old Testament but also to develop an anti-Semitic bias. Unfortunately, some Christians who follow this thinking have become prejudiced against Jews.[8]

In a similar discussion of African American systematic theology, James H. Evans discusses the variety of christological approaches that tend to trivialize the Hebrew Bible and, subsequently, Jewish beliefs of the intertestamental period. Evans urges what he identifies as a "figural" approach, where Jesus Christ is a "figura" or model of liberator. According to Evans, Jesus as figura refers "to both the reflection of something that already existed, as well as the projection of something yet to be...Jesus Christ was a figura in the sense that he was a cosmic projection of 'the new Adam,' the image of God restored to its original state, as well as the historical projection of liberated humanity."[9] Evans surveys the "Black Christ" options in the work of James Cone, J. DeOtis Roberts, and Albert Cleage, and promotes this metaphorical or imagistic way of interpreting Christ in order to overcome what he believes to be theological problems with opposing Jesus (and Christianity) to the faith of the Hebrew Bible.

---

[8]J. Alfred Smith, Jr., *New Treasures from the Old: A Guide to Preaching from the Old Testament* (Progressive National Baptist Convention, 1987), 17.

[9]James H. Evans, Jr., *We Have Been Believers: An African American Systematic Theology* (Minneapolis: Fortress Press, 1992), 78.

Thus, figura—with its connotations of the changing aspects of the permanent, its ability to refer to novelty and continuity, and its capacity to embrace both the spiritual and the historical dimensions of persons and events—proved an apt vehicle for expressing the relation between the Mosaic roots of Israel's faith, the messianic expectations of the prophets, and the christological claims of the early Christian community.[10]

M. Shawn Copeland, womanist theologian, also identifies anti-Semitism (which is not identical to anti-Judaism, but functions similarly in Christian rhetoric) as a theological problem of interest to womanist scholars in religion. "It seems to me that black feminists and/or womanists seek a new and common ground from which all women and men may vigorously oppose racism, sexism, homophobia, ageism, class exploitation, intentional limitation of the disabled, and—I add, as Christians must—anti-Semitism."[11]

Homiletic scholars John Holbert and Ronald J. Allen have written extensively about the way such anti-Jewish prejudices or exclusive christologies are sponsored or promoted through preaching. Holbert is a Hebrew Bible scholar and homiletician, while Allen is a New Testament scholar and homiletician. Their work surveys a variety of hermeneutical approaches used in preaching, ranging from models of complete discontinuity between the testaments to models of continuity. The most common hermeneutical/homiletical model is the "uniqueness" option identified by Smith, which tends to elevate the Newer Testament over the First and argues for a relationship that either rejects the Hebrew Bible or subordinates it to the Christian writings, granting ultimate authority to the Christian version.

First, we will deal with the most adversarial models, in which the First Testament is characterized in such a way as to be rejected. One is the *law/gospel model*, in which the Older Testament is portrayed negatively as a canon of law, while the Newer Testament is portrayed positively as canon of mercy. In this approach, the law functions to convict of us our sinfulness and our human frailty; it is a set of rules (works) by which to gain God's favor. The law/gospel paradigm typically characterizes Israel as works-oriented, meticulously following rules by which to secure righteousness before God. The gospel, in contrast, sets us free from the bondage to law since Christ both fulfills the law and renders

---

[10]Evans, *We Have Been Believers*, 78. See also Kelly Brown Douglas's work on christology, *The Black Christ* (Maryknoll, N. Y.: Orbis Books, 1998).

[11]M. Shawn Copeland, "Christian Ethics and Theology in Womanist Perspective," *Journal of Feminist Studies in Religion*, 5, no. 2, (Fall 1989): 99–100.

it meaningless. The language of old/new covenant or old/new dispensation derives from this opposition of law to gospel. Homiletically the law/gospel paradigm casts Israel as legalistic and misguided, a community of believers who "anxiously try to fulfill the impossible."[12]

Variations on this adversarial approach include characterizations of the relationship between the testaments as an *external/internal dichotomy,* suggesting that the Older Testament deals primarily with concerns of the flesh and the things of the world, while the Newer Testament deals with internal spiritual matters. Another variation on the adversarial approach characterizes the faith of Israel as exclusively ethnic, in contrast to the universality of the church. This *ethnic Israel/Universal Church* model usually contrasts the idea of election or chosenness (Israel) with the lack of regard for ethnic status attributed to Christianity (neither Jew nor Gentile, etc.).

Slightly more benevolent subordination paradigms value the Hebrew Bible, but only grant it a partial or derivative value. One familiar "weak subordination" strategy is the *prophecy-fulfillment paradigm,* which interprets the Older Testament as a kind of promissory note that is decisively redeemed in the person of Jesus. Within this approach the Older Testament is cast in the role of Christ's herald or forerunner and the Hebrew Bible has a certain derivative value for foretelling the future. Another popular strategy is the *typology approach,* which finds "correspondences between past events, practices, institutions, or persons" to interpret present or future events and persons.[13] Typology can be a legitimate and helpful way to understand the ongoing shaping of a tradition, but can easily be distorted to reduce previous events and persons to little more than prophetic foreshadowing. Typological approaches frequently give way to allegorical approaches where earlier events and figures have no intrinsic value, but only take meaning when interpreted from some vantage point external to the primitive story. "The elements of the text are often read as symbols of true meaning that can be discerned only when one has the key to the meaning of the symbols."[14] All the weaker subordination approaches find value in the Old Testament, but tend to reduce its meaning to nothing more than prelude for the New Testament.

---

[12]John C. Holbert and Ronald J. Allen, *Holy Root, Holy Branches: Christian Preaching from the Old Testament* (Nashville: Abingdon Press, 1995), 18. The discussion here follows Holbert's and Allen's characterizations of typical approaches, 15–31.

[13]Holbert and Allen, *Holy Root, Holy Branches,* 24. See also J. Alfred Smith's comments on typology, *New Treasures from the Old,* 33–35.

[14]Ibid., 23.

The *continuity approach* does not subordinate one testament to another, nor does it argue for evolutionary progress in theological meaning. A theology of continuity assumes that the same God is operating in both histories, for the same purposes, through the same kinds of agents. The continuity model is the one suggested by Evans in his discussion of the "figura" approach. Such an approach recognizes that both testaments contain claims of God's unconditional mercy right along with a theology of merit or works-righteousness. If the relationship between the two testaments is continuous, we will not expect to find Jews contrasted to Christians, Jesus contrasted to Moses, or the temple contrasted to the contemporary church. A theology of continuity presents challenges for more traditional christologies that prefer to argue for special revelation in Jesus or for the uniqueness of Jesus. A continuity or compatibilty model calls for a theology of the gospel that is not derived from any special claims about the person of Jesus or of unique salvation. It tends to couch christological claims in ways that call into question certain Second Testament claims along with some First Testament claims. It also tends to call into question certain traditional orthodoxies and creedal affirmations. The continuity approach opens up the possibility that revelation is ongoing and subject to challenge and interpretation.

Continuity approaches are frequently grounded in human hopes for a better historical future and the confidence that God's purposes always point in the direction of abundant life for all. Both testaments witness to an eschatological hope, an ultimate fulfillment of the promises made throughout both faith traditions. The elements of prophecy/fulfillment, when applied uniformly throughout both testaments, attest to the fact that "God's promises for ultimate justice in every realm have not come to full and complete manifestation" either in Israel's history or the church's history.[15] "In the most anguished and profound sense, both Judaism and Christianity continue to yearn for the coming of eschatological shalom."[16] Continuity or compatibility models lean more toward emphasizing the goodness of the good news, rather than its novelty.

We will explore each homiletic theory for its assumptions about the relationship between the testaments and the way gospel formulations argue for continuity or discontinuity between Judaism and Christianity.

---

[15]Ibid., 27.
[16]Ibid., 27.

One of the most interesting aspects of this question, particularly for African American homiletics, is the way the homiletical oral tradition has interpreted the exodus event and the figure of Moses, as well as other heroic figures from the First Testament.[17]

Nature and Purpose of Faith Communities

Ecclesiology, or the nature of the church, is not always an immediate consideration for homiletic theorists. Homileticians tend to think first of the nature of the sermonic content (whether theological or biblical content) and how that content will best be offered for the hearers. However, we've already noticed that assumptions about the purpose of preaching also imply assumptions about the rhetorical context of the preaching event. If, for example, one homiletic purpose is to convict sinners of their guilt, we've already made assumptions about rhetorical context. We assume something about our audience, namely that they are sinners in need of salvation. Preachers make implicit assumptions all the time about their hearers, what they want or need, and what the preacher considers most appropriate to those situations.

Even though homiletic theory almost always assumes something about the greater purposes of the church, relatively little attention has been given to the relationship between homiletic theory and the broader corporate vocation or identity of the community of believers. Within Euro-American homiletic studies, some postliberal scholars follow Stanley Hauerwas and George Lindbeck and argue for cultural-linguistic communities of character, or peculiar communities whose identities are in contrast to contemporary culture: resident aliens.[18] Others argue for a different understanding of the communal vocation or identity of the church, claiming that the church is not peculiar by its own internal character, but by its vocational orientation toward embracing the world that God so loves. David Buttrick is one of this latter group, chastising

---

[17]Without making the theological distinctions or arguments that I propose here, Renita Weems has actually demonstrated the continuity approach in her work on female figures from the First Testament. See the "Further Reading" list for chapter 7 on "African American Women and Womanists" for suggestions relative to Weems's work.

[18]Stanley Hauerwas, *A Community of Character* (South Bend, Ind.: University of Notre Dame Press, 1988); Stanley Hauerwas and William Willimon, *Resident Aliens: Life in the Christian Colony* (Nashville: Abingdon Press, 1989); Stanley Hauerwas, *Unleashing the Scripture: Freeing the Bible from Captivity to America* (Nashville: Abingdon Press, 1993); George A. Lindbeck, *The Nature of Doctrine: Religion and Theology in a Postliberal Age* (Philadelphia: Westminster Press, 1984); George A. Lindbeck, *The Nature of Confession: Evangelicals and Postliberals in Conversation,* ed. Timothy R. Phillips and Dennis L. Okholm (Downers Grove, Ill.: InterVarsity Press, 1996).

the contemporary church for its bunker mentality and calling it to be an agent of grace and promise in the world. He refers to the church as the "being-saved" community, whose mission is Christ's mission of prophetic activity, justice-oriented ministry, and ultimately, reconciliation. In Buttrick's model, the purpose of preaching is not for confessional identity or church growth or institutional management, but to continue the preaching of Christ that sets us free for neighbor-love, manifested as social justice.

Again, LaRue's work is an exception within studies of African American homiletics. His is one of the few homiletical voices calling for sustained attention to corporate and communal issues related to preaching. LaRue identifies what he calls "domains of experience," or "the tangible, corporeal situations in which the sovereign God's power is sought and demonstrated in the life experiences of blacks."[19] Where other African American scholars have attempted to argue that social justice issues have primacy in the tradition's preaching, LaRue indicates a much broader actual spectrum of experiential or "audience" concerns. He identifies five such domains as dynamics of a black biblical hermeneutic: personal piety, care of the soul, social justice, corporate concerns, and institutional maintenance of the church.[20]

Personal piety is the most common domain, emphasizing "'heart religion,' the centrality of the Bible for faith and life, the royal priesthood of the laity, and strict morality."[21] Other dimensions of personal piety concern emotional response, suspicion of appeals to reason, and an evangelical rebirth or conversion experience.[22] *Care of the soul* focuses on the well-being of individuals and frequently includes assumptions about personal wholeness, healing, grief, and the challenges that believers experience as a result of prejudice and discrimination. It would be consistent with LaRue's interpretation to observe that care of the soul frequently makes use of psychological categories and values as they are appropriated theologically.[23] *Social justice* concerns are that domain that attends to matters of the social world and the need for social reform. Within social justice concerns one might include observations about racism, sexism, sexual orientation, and economic and political realities. The aim of social justice preaching is to bring about constructive

---

[19]LaRue, *The Heart of Black Preaching*, 20.
[20]Ibid., 20–25.
[21]Ibid., 21.
[22]Ibid.
[23]Ibid., 22.

social change.[24] *Corporate concerns* could be characterized as observations and critiques internal to the African American community. If social justice preaching addresses issues of change beyond the black community, corporate concerns tend to center on themes of self-help, uplift, and racial solidarity. "Unlike the domain of social justice, which seeks the common good of all, the corporate concerns domain is specifically geared to black interests."[25] While LaRue doesn't make this specific connection, the current social phenomena of "F.U.B.U." or "for us, by us" is a cultural manifestation of this theological articulation that African Americans should exercise social and economic power that benefits their own community. He does cite the Million Man March and the move toward racially segregated education as examples. *Institutional maintenance of the church* is the last domain treated by LaRue. This domain "has more to do with ethos than with specific acts" and is concerned with preserving the autonomy and viability of the institution that has afforded African Americans a consistent venue for fellowship, self-identity, and self-respect. Within this domain, preachers give "continued life and sustenance to the institutional church, which in turn reaffirms and upholds its participants."[26]

Regardless of the diversity within either African American or white homiletic approaches, the reigning paradigms tend to favor either an individualistic model (personal piety) or an institutional maintenance model. LaRue confirms that African American preaching tends to sponsor personal piety and institutional maintenance above other concerns. LaRue does not take an evaluative position on this reality, but merely reports it to be the case within African American preaching. What LaRue's work suggests is that a claim for "social justice concerns" as a primary homiletical issue within African American preaching is simply not borne out in a survey of sermons.

There is probably true common ground here between African American and white homiletics, since neither tradition offers sustained homiletical reflection on what preaching does to form the church for its ministry of justice within the broader world.[27] Whether we assume that preaching saves souls, nurtures psyches, or teaches doctrine, the dominant homiletic models call for preaching that is directed toward

---

[24]Ibid., 22–23.

[25]Ibid., 23.

[26]Ibid., 25.

[27]I recognize that this is not the common ground that most African American and Euro-American homileticians would prefer to acknowledge. Such a sobering observation should do *exactly* that: sober us.

individual persons or a narrow communal identity, on the assumption that our own constituents are the ultimate beneficiaries. In this approach, our sermons are addressed to personal anxiety, existential doubt, or personal failure, calling (usually) for some new insight or identity that allows each to function as a whole person again. Sermon illustrations are most likely to be vignettes about individuals, whether in the "before" or "after" mode, and frequently feature a tragic/heroic type: a sports figure, a cancer victim, a retarded child, Mother Teresa, Martin Luther King, Jr., and so on. Sin and salvation are regularly imaged as the personal activities of a solo character. Specifically within African American homiletic strategies, the solo "exemplar types" are frequently biblical characters or individuals from popular black culture.[28]

The individual model for homiletics (personal piety or care of the soul) has dominated for so long that other options are sometimes difficult to imagine. However, ritual studies, sociological studies, and rhetorical studies are beginning to have an impact on homiletic theory. These three disciplines contribute different understandings of the way groups form, negotiate meaning, and cooperate in shared projects. Ritual theory is concerned with symbolic activity and the way groups are transformed into intentional communities of shared practice. Sociological studies help shift the attention from individual psychology to group psychology, to study the way groups negotiate their relationships, handle conflict, and develop cooperative strategies. The study of rhetoric involves the way oral discourse constructs an argument strategy to persuade not just individuals but groups toward corporate activity. Some homiletic theories are beginning to appropriate understandings from these three disciplines to inform the way that preaching uses symbolic language and persuasive strategies, within a ritual setting, for community formation and commitment to shared projects.[29] Rather than promoting highly psychologized images of individualism, homileticians are learning to promote images of highly diverse yet committed communities, engaged in real interaction with one another and the world.[30] These approaches do not ask how the gospel addresses questions

---

[28]Again, see James Evans's discussion of "figura" or heroic types within the African American tradition in *We Have Been Believers*, 80.

[29]Evans Crawford's work with Thomas H. Troeger, *The Hum: Call and Response in African American Preaching* (Nashville: Abingdon Press, 1995) is an exciting work for this reason. See a longer treatment of Crawford's work in chapter 6.

[30]Within African American homiletic thought, this trajectory is emerging among womanist and black feminist scholars and preachers. See chapter 7 on African American women and womanists.

of generic individual meaning (Who am I in relationship to God and in relationship to the world?), but how the gospel addresses questions of faithful communities in action (Who are we as a faith community, and how do we relate to God and the world?).

All these considerations relate not only to the identity or various identities of the hearers but to their understandings of responsible activity. In more familiar language, this is the question of the mission of the church. Four broad orientations can be identified, and each has implications for homiletic theory.

In a *sanctuary orientation,* the congregation understands itself in highly spiritualized ways, perhaps with an otherworldly emphasis, to exist primarily to provide its membership with opportunities to withdraw from the problems of daily life and take temporary respite in a community of like-minded individuals.[31] Within contemporary homiletic theory (whether African American or white), this orientation draws heavily on a pastoral therapeutic interpretation, offering consolation and emotional safety to its members. Metaphors of family, intimacy, healing, and comfort tend to dominate preaching and rhetoric, encouraging a distinction between the religious community and the world. A sanctuary church tends to have a negative evaluation of secular culture. The rhetorical attempts to disassociate the believers from the world range from radical sectarianism to mild opposition. A sanctuary church encourages members to resist the temptation of contemporary lifestyles and pleasures, to defer pleasure for a distant (otherworldly) reward, to accept one's earthly status and situation, and to exercise religious duty primarily as individuals who are kind, law-abiding, and patriotic.

An *evangelistic orientation* to the church's mission in the world assumes that the church's primary function is to convert unbelievers to the faith. The world is devalued in and of itself in favor of the world to come. Evangelistic churches promote active study and witness, proselytizing among other religious groups, protecting members from false teaching, and preparing members for the (otherworldly) world to come. The spirit of the great commission is at the center of congregational life, and where church members are explicitly urged to have contact with the world, it is for the purposes of drawing others out of the world and into the evangelistic fold. Evangelistic churches interact with the world to offer spiritual salvation, but are rarely concerned with issues of social justice and liberation.

---

[31]These four orientations are drawn from Jackson Carroll, Carl S. Dudley, and William McKinney, eds., *Handbook for Congregational Studies* (Nashville: Abingdon Press, 1986), 29–31.

Civic congregations orient toward the world with more concern for social justice issues, but encourage members to act as individuals for these purposes. They tend to encourage cooperation with other agencies and faith communities to promote service to the needy; they tend to trust existing structures and hesitate to challenge them. Civic models of mission operate on the model of individual citizenship, equipping individuals to see themselves as agents of God's love. Civic congregations may provide a forum for debating social issues and exploring responsible strategies, but usually stop short of advocating a specific ethical posture. The civic church resists acting as a corporate body in the public, but instead encourages its members to make their own faith decisions and act on them individually.

The *activist ecclesial model* understands its mission as the direct promotion and support of corporate participation in social and political issues. Social change is advocated through organized, direct, and collective influence. The congregation sponsors social action groups within the congregation, encourages its pastor to speak out publicly on specific social and political issues, and provides financial support for sustained advocacy. The activist orientation assumes that the world is God's arena and that the church is called to be an advocate for the world that God loves. Social justice, social critique, and proactive challenge to existing economic and political structures are high priorities for bringing about a world transformed toward God's intentions. The focus is dominantly this-worldly, prophetic, and collective. The difference between the civic model and the activist model can be summed up in the words of an early feminist writer: "We have to quit concentrating on pulling drowning women out of the river. Someone has to go upstream and stop them from throwing women in."[32] While we don't have to oppose the two strategies, we might at least want to recognize the different goals and methods of each position, the difference between prevention and rescue.

Homiletic theory, whether explicitly or implicitly, sponsors an orientation to congregational expectations and activities. Understandings of the good news and of the purpose of preaching itself provide foundations for an ecclesial theology and an understanding of the church's primary purpose. Part of our survey will attend to the assumptions about the nature and purpose of faith communities as

---

[32]I have been unable to locate the source of this saying. It's possible that it's simply part of the early white feminist oral tradition.

these assumptions are sponsored by particular theological claims and methodological strategies.

Preaching and Liturgy

Since most preaching occurs within a regular liturgical context and among a community of baptized believers, the assumed relationship between preaching and the rest of the regular order of service can be instructive. While none of the homileticians surveyed come from what we might consider to be a "high" liturgical tradition, these assumptions will most likely be dealt with indirectly, if at all. For example, Evans Crawford's *The Hum* uses ritual theory assumptions to discuss the way that call-and-response patterns form congregations for their shared projects. Without making overt connections, Crawford does in fact imply a continuity between preaching and the rest of the liturgical context, suggesting that joint recitation and participation have an impact on how theological meaning is negotiated and shared. To use other examples, James Forbes makes more explicit connections between preaching and the sacraments as mutual means of grace. James Massey's attention to the relationship between preaching and Christ's presence provides the groundwork for eucharist to be construed as a means of grace and a way of encountering the divine. Henry Mitchell's attention to celebration in preaching offers an implicit connection to the celebration of the eucharist and the way that corporate delight reinforces theological appropriations.

We will attend to liturgical and sacramental matters both from the perspective of ritual theory and from the perspective of sacramental theology. It's fair to say that among the Baptist homileticians, the focus on baptismal theology and its connection to preaching assumes a higher profile, and that among those in the Wesleyan tradition, eucharistic theology is a more figural partner.

Racial Orientation and African American Studies

A broad spectrum of orientations toward racial identity exists within African American homiletic theories. Stretching back to early slave preachers and to the beginnings of the institutional black church, we can trace both overt and covert liberation themes. Among some of the educated antebellum and postbellum free black preachers, themes of nationalism and Pan-African identity surfaced. Some of the most vocal social protest of the nineteenth century originated from the African

American pulpit, from such figures as Alexander Crummell, Henry McNeal Turner, Henry Highland Garnet, Jarena Lee, Zilpha Elaw, Julia Foote, and Nannie Helen Burroughs.[33]

By the beginning of the twentieth century, however, the failure of Reconstruction and the accompanying social protest had largely given way to more immediate matters of survival in a changing economic reality. Black populations were largely displaced from agricultural to urban contexts, and churches assumed an enormous burden of providing for the survival of constituents. Churches became social safety nets, offering education, medical care, and financial support for an increasingly displaced population. Self-help operated at the level of individual congregations, and, increasingly, at a level of more organized agencies and organizations within the African American community.[34] Gayraud Wilmore argues that the radical strain of African American discourse and practice has always been present even within the most "survivalist" periods of African American religious history. What this project argues is consistent with Wilmore's interpretation that certain modes emerge as dominant in certain periods.

Within the first two decades of the twentieth century, two African American leaders of national stature—W. E. B. DuBois and Booker T. Washington—arose with competing theories on how to lift African Americans from their status as second-class citizens.[35] As a theme in African American cultural and religious life, *uplift* refers to self-help strategies for improving the social conditions of persons of color within a dominant white culture. The origins of the uplift theme probably occured prior to the twentieth century, but became figural during the

---

[33]See Marcia Riggs's work on African American women in religious history in *Can I Get a Witness: Prophetic Religious Voices of African American Women, an Anthology* (Maryknoll, N.Y.: Orbis Books, 1997).

[34]Every attempt at historical interpretation is subject to debate. This project is primarily informed by Gayraud Wilmore, *Black Religion and Black Radicalism: An Interpretation of the Religious History of African Americans* (Maryknoll, N.Y.: Orbis Books, 1989); Joseph Washington, *Black Sects and Cults* (Garden City, N.Y.: Doubleday, 1972); and A. H. Fauset, *Black Gods of the Metropolis: Negro Religious Cults of the Urban North* (New York: Octagon Books, 1970). Wilmore's work is probably the most contentious, since it neither favors an interpretation of a major radical tradition, nor completely diminishes the radical strains within more "survivalist" periods. It is probably the case that Wilmore's attempts to periodicize African American religious history along the continuum of "radical" and "survivalist" has generated the most debate.

[35]It's beyond the scope of this project to consider all the major figures and movements, but I should at least make mention of Marcus Garvey's UNIA project, one of the most ambitious programs in African American modern history. Garvey organized a massive "back-to-Africa" project, promoted black pride, and organized schools, hospitals, and financial institutions that were wholly black-owned and -operated. While impressive, Garvey's movement was short-lived and lacked overall support from the black community.

early controversies between DuBois and Washington.[36] Uplift themes and concerns are probably most accurately connected with what Cleophus LaRue has characterized as "corporate concerns."

Washington believed that African Americans would achieve success and be accepted into white dominant society by gradually becoming economically valuable. His strategy was to promote extensive vocational education for African Americans, to train them to be useful in contemporary American life. He was a gradualist, advocating that social change would occur slowly and through increased economic equity. While he was certainly not opposed to higher formal education, he was adamant that vocational education was the first step toward higher education programs at some future time.

DuBois was also a gradualist, but a political gradualist.[37] He believed that the key to uplifting the race was for African Americans to assume more and more political power, and that such a goal could only be accomplished through the education of "the talented tenth" of the population that could benefit from higher education. DuBois believed that as many African Americans as possible should be educated for the professions: medicine, law, teaching. DuBois considered Washington to be too much of a compromiser, too concerned about upsetting whites, and too willing to settle for deferred equal status.

Both these uplift ideologies were operative throughout the early part of the century, during the formation of the NAACP, the Urban League, and other guilds and philanthropic endeavors. They were not overt protest movements, but strategies whereby the African American community could lift itself up from the legacy of slavery and oppression. The role of the church shifted from its nineteenth-century forms of social protest and outspoken leadership to more social conformity with white churches, albeit with the additional "social safety net" burden toward its members. The social conformity or "move to the socio-theological middle" should not be understood as an imitation or accommodation with white Christianity, but as an attempt to adjust to emerging urban realities and to foster the stability of the institutional black church.[38]

---

[36]For a discussion of the earlier history of uplift ideology, see Edward L. Wheeler, *Uplifting the Race: The Black Minister in the New South 1865-1902* (Lanham, Md.: University Press of America, 1986).

[37]Manning Marable chronicles the nuances and shifts in DuBoisian thought, demonstrating that DuBois had a significant radical impulse. See Manning Marable, *W.E.B. DuBois: Black Radical Democrat* (Boston: Twayne, 1986).

[38]Wilmore, *Black Religion and Black Radicalism*, 160–66.

Within a period of less than twenty years, popular leadership styles within the African American community changed from an activist posture promoted largely by black preachers (Henry McNeal Turner's polemic against lynching, which recommended that "negroes get guns"[39]) to gradualist postures promoted by intellectual leaders. Booker T. Washington's conciliatory Atlanta Compromise (1895) called for gradual accommodation within vocational education and economic structures, while DuBois called for political advances and higher education.

Clergy *generally* followed the trend away from protest and activism. Ministers *generally* assumed the mantle of local leadership and public interpretation, whether sympathetic to Washingtonian or DuBoisian ideals. Wilmore refers to this period as the "deradicalization" of the black church, which corresponded with the rise of the black bourgeoisie and the "Great Migration" of African Americans into the cities of the North.[40] Many of the older male homileticians in this current study were born during the early part of the twentieth century, were culturally and theologically formed by implicit theories of uplifting the race, and developed pastoral leadership styles that exercised some degree of gradualism or accommodation with the larger white culture. Black radicalism and protest movements were largely displaced from the church in the first half of the twentieth century, and instead found their niche within nonreligious communities.

The activities of Martin Luther King, Jr., and the Southern Christian Leadership Conference during the era of civil rights renewed impulses of African American protest within the church, but without the adversarial tone characterized by the nineteenth-century preachers. King did not emerge from the African American church without immediate precedent, however. Much of the groundwork for King's protest movement was actually laid by Vernon Johns, his immediate predecessor at Dexter Avenue Baptist Church in Montgomery, Alabama. Johns was an outspoken critic of segregation, often taking his theological interpretations public, both in speech and action. The Sunday morning after a Ku Klux Klan cross was burned in the Dexter churchyard, Johns preached on "the lynching of Jesus" in a sermon titled "It's Safe to Murder Negroes

---

[39]Henry McNeal Turner, *Voice of Missions,* March-May, 1897.
[40]Wilmore, *Black Religion and Black Radicalism,* 135ff.

in Montgomery." When King arrived at Dexter Avenue, he did so on Johns's legacy.[41]

King and the SCLC built their endeavors on certain implicit assumptions of the middle-class church and its leadership styles, moving into the public with critique, but with an ongoing commitment to integration and the ideals of American democracy. Where earlier preachers had advocated for a separate church and a separate nation, King and his followers were committed to the ideal of a unified American public that included African Americans in "the dream." Again, where there was adversarial or separatist polemic, it came primarily from outside the black church, most notably in the work of Malcolm X and the more politically militant Student Non-Violent Coordinating Committee. Many of the older homileticians in this book were contemporaries of King, and more sympathetic to his "agape" style of persuasion and his hopes for a "beloved community." Like King, they were college-educated primarily in African American institutions of higher education with close ties to the historic black church, even as many pursued graduate education in predominantly white or more racially diverse institutions.

James H. Cone is a watershed figure, not only for theological education concerns but for our current consideration of the leadership styles and assumptions of a new era of African American homileticians. Cone received his undergraduate education at Philander Smith College, a historically African American, Methodist-affiliated college in Little Rock, Arkansas; his graduate education was in predominantly white institutions. He received his B.D. from Garrett Theological Seminary in 1961; his M.A. and Ph.D. from Northwestern University, in 1963 and 1965, respectively. Cone is an ordained minister in the African Methodist Episcopal Church. Cone was part of the first generation of black scholars to attend college and seminary during and after the civil rights movement.

---

[41]Taylor Branch, *Parting the Waters: America in the King Years 1954–63* (New York: Simon & Schuster, 1988), 1–26. See also Richard Lischer's exceptional work on King and the Johns precedent, *The Preacher King: Martin Luther King, Jr. and the Word That Moved America* (New York: Oxford University Press, 1995), 74–77. Lewis Baldwin, Jr., has written about King as a product of the African American church and culture in *There is a Balm in Gilead: The Cultural Roots of Martin Luther King, Jr.* (Minneapolis: Fortress Press, 1991); *To Make the Wounded Whole: The Cultural Legacy of Martin Luther King, Jr.* (Minneapolis: Fortress Press, 1992); and *Toward the Beloved Community: Martin Luther King, Jr. and South Africa* (Cleveland: Pilgrim Press, 1995).

Cone was influenced by the work of Albert Cleage, whose *The Black Messiah* (New York: Sheed and Ward, 1968) reopened the tradition of black Christian radicalism. While Cone didn't follow Cleage's assumptions of a Christ who was physically black, he did call for a God on the side of the oppressed and an "ontologically" black Christ. Cone became a key figure in formulating a new synthesis between African American Christianity and Black Power movements to inaugurate Black Theology. Where earlier theologians and pastors had promoted integration and the dream of a "color-blind" society, Cone and his colleagues promoted racial pride and a Black Theology of liberation, calling Western theological traditions into question, along with white interpretive approaches to scripture. For Cone, biblical faith was best understood in light of African American struggles against oppression and injustice. His book *Black Theology and Black Power* (New York: Seabury Press, 1969) was the seminal publication inaugurating the Black Theology Project. With subsequent publications, particularly *The Spirituals and the Blues* (New York: Seabury Press, 1972), Cone encouraged a self-conscious racial identification, drawing on African American tradition as a theological resource.

The implications for homiletic theory are significant. Prior to the Black Theology Project of Cone and other sympathetic theologians, homiletic theory among African American scholars did not explicitly attend to the theological implications of social context, to theological solidarity on behalf of the oppressed, or to constructive methods that honored the particularity of being African American. Prior to Cone, we do not see a public African American homiletic theory that is self-consciously located within the black church or community.

Martin Luther King, Jr., himself admitted that he was embarrassed in his early preaching career to "preach black" or to make use of African American homiletic conventions such as "black English," alliteration, emotionalism, or "whooping." King was not alone in his assumptions that preachers should "uplift" the congregation through scrupulous grammar, careful elocution, and impressive vocabulary. The other "gentlemen preachers" of his generation had similar commitments to a particular leadership style that manifested itself in sermons according to what Augustine called the "grand" or "inspirational" style of rhetoric. Sermon illustrations came from Western literary traditions, from Western philosophy, from Western poetry, and from the sciences. Rhetorical style was marked more by dignity and the kind of "authorities" valued by white homiletical standards.

After Cone, homiletic theory among African Americans took a decided turn, reclaiming African roots in content and in style.[42] The grand and eloquent rhetorical style of older homileticians was considered to be less authentic to African roots and to contemporary African American experience. The same way that natural hairstyles and daishiki shirts became more popular within youth culture, a "natural" and Afrocentric style of preaching gained homiletical authority. "No Black man can truly identify with a God who speaks only the language of the white oppressor. A Black rendition of scripture does in language what a Black Christ or a Black Madonna does in art. God is divested of his 'proper,' white, socially distant role, a personification of deity completely outside Black culture and life."[43] Homileticians were more likely to promote the intentional use of vernacular or black English, to promote idiomatic language, to profile African American heroes, to encourage call-and-response rhetorical "prompts," to promote sermon structures culminating in celebration, and to engage in critiques of racism from a theological perspective.[44] It is also significant that a number of womanist theologians who are contributing to homiletic theory were either directly trained by James H. Cone or have been influenced by his work in the Black Theology Project.

Preaching and Language Studies

Several of the scholars we will survey have been, explicitly or implicitly, influenced by changing understandings of language and language theory. According to Joseph M. Webb, the twentieth century experienced a quiet revolution in the study and understanding of language.[45] Older positivist approaches, inherited from the Enlightenment and from rationalism, were called into question as

---

[42]See a discussion of Afrocentric preaching themes prior to Cone's work in Janice Denise Hamlet, "Religious Discourse as Cultural Narrative: A Critical Analysis of the Rhetoric of African-American Sermons" (Ph.D. diss., Ohio State University, 1989).

[43]Henry M. Mitchell, *Black Preaching* (New York: Harper & Row, 1970), 155.

[44]In some ways, Mitchell was part of a broad homiletic movement in the early 1970s that gave sustained attention to language and to the hearers. Fred Craddock's watershed book *As One Without Authority* was published in 1971, and it recommended moving away from "lecture-style" preaching that featured heavy exposition and rational "point-making" structures. See chapter 6 on Henry H. Mitchell for further discussion of his black cultural approach to homiletics.

[45]I'll borrow heavily from Joseph M. Webb's discussion of the six major shifts in language studies in the twentieth century in *Old Texts, New Sermons: The Quiet Revolution in Biblical Preaching* (St. Louis: Chalice Press, 2000). There are other excellent discussions of these shifts and their implications for homiletic theory. David Buttrick's work offers similar interpretations, as does the work of Richard Eslinger and others. Webb's discussion is brief and conveniently organized.

Shifts came from many directions and out of numerous intellectual orientations–psychology, sociology, literary and political criticism, the pedagogies of reading and learning, anthropology, ethnography, linguistics, semantics, semiotics, and information theory–all disciplines (along with some others) that made their contributions to a profoundly changed view of the nature of language; how it is acquired and how it is used in an untold number of ways.[46]

The primary challenge was to the standard communication theory, which assumes that there is a message, a sender, and a receiver. In this model, the preacher's purpose is to package the message (usually distilled from a text by some process) clearly so the receiver receives it relatively "pure" in its original meaning. The communication model tends to give primary attention to single words or concepts as if they can be studied (note the scientific method presumed?) in isolation from their other linguistic signifiers.

One of the earliest challenges to this communication model came from Ferdinand de Saussure, whose works from early in the century were being translated into English. De Saussure's linguistic theory claimed that words do not have meaning in and of themselves, isolated from their relation to other words, whether in a sentence or a larger unit. The relationship between a single word and its referent was arbitrary, something socially negotiated through its relationship to other words. Language, according to de Saussure, is culturally based. "Words meant what they did, whether individually or in various combinations, because the individuals who comprised a particular culture agreed, and agreed over time, that those words should mean those particular things."[47] De Saussure's claim about the arbitrariness of language suggests that we are unable to discern the precise meaning of a particular word or concept (especially related to ancient texts). This calls one-to-one word translation into question, but also, more fundamentally, whether historical critical work is as useful in exegesis and getting "behind" a text as had been previously thought, especially where such one-to-one correspondence has been assumed. For preachers, this was not only a question of biblical hermeneutics but a critical question of the language used in preaching. If our preacher language is arbitrary, socially negotiated, and open to new meaning, with what

[46]Webb, *Old Texts, New Sermons,* 1–2.
[47]Ibid., 3. See Ferdinand de Saussure, *Course in General Linguistics* (New York: McGraw-Hill, 1965).

confidence do we presume to bring a word from God? And with what confidence do we declare that any particular meaning is more valid than another? De Saussure's work called into question the "objectivity" of biblical language studies.

Another challenge to objectivity and the positivist approach was the rhetoricians' claims that all language is loaded. Amos Wilder was a key figure in biblical literary studies, claiming that there was something different in the way the gospel writers themselves used language. Wilder connected certain ways of using language to certain theological and ethical agendas. We use different kinds of language for different purposes: concrete language for action, dreamy language for visionary images, loaded language all around. Wilder was attentive to how early Christian rhetoric worked to convey its meaning and to the oral speech patterns and rhetorical tactics that lay behind their writings.[48]

For example, my saying "she cut his throat" is rhetorically different from saying "she slit his gullet" or "she drew a sharp instrument across the flesh of his neck." The more loaded phrase is the middle one, "she slit his gullet," since it captures a sense of crudeness and suddenness that the other two do not. The third option may pretend to be more objective language, suggesting a certain emotional detachment, both in the act of throat-cutting and in the preacher's relation to the topic of gullet-slitting. Notice, though, that feigning objectivity about gullet-slitting is certainly a loaded perspective in and of itself.[49] Not only are there no objective solo words, but there are no objective combinations. In fact, the combination with other words makes any particular word more and more loaded, as certain interpretations are excluded and certain ones promoted, simply by the selection of adjacent words (as with my selection of gullet and slit). Kenneth Burke refers to these as "terministic screens" that direct the hearers' attention toward the speaker's agenda.[50]

---

[48]Amos N. Wilder, *Early Christian Rhetoric* (Cambridge, Mass.: Harvard University Press, 1964; reissue, 1971), cited in Richard Lischer, *Theories of Preaching: Selected Readings in the Homiletical Tradition* (Durham, N.C.: Labyrinth Press, 1987), 237.

[49]Feigning objectivity is one of the key "myths" of the Eurocentric tradition, according to Henry Mitchell. See the discussion of Mitchell's interpretations of language in chapter 6.

[50]Kenneth Burke, "Terministic Screens," in his *Language as Symbolic Action: Essays on Life, Literature and Method* (Berkeley and Los Angeles: University of California Press, 1966), cited in Webb, *Old Texts, New Sermons*, 4. Katie Cannon's writing on language, metaphor, and the presence of certain themes assumes the Burkian assumptions about terministic screens. Insights from Teresa Fry Brown (on the social construction of black women), from Cheryl Gilkes (on masculine and feminine images for God), and from Cheryl Sanders (on homiletic "tasks" evident in African American women's preaching) likewise bear out Burke's theories of terministic screening that direct attention toward or away from certain theological values. As a whole, the womanist trajectory of contemporary theological and homiletical studies attends more to language issues than does the male trajectory.

I. A. Richards is another rhetorician who challenged the communication theory, or what he called the "Proper Meaning Superstition." Richards calls for the "interinanimation" of meaning, claiming that words animate one another through their interactions, not through their individual or inherent meanings. In his organic understanding of language, Richards claims that a single word is capable of "beguiling" other words in the utterance.[51]

These new insights into language contribute to a third claim, namely that language has persuasive power and that speakers intend for hearers to hear in certain ways. Once we believe that the use of language is persuasive or rhetorical, we challenge an older assumption that language use is primarily expressive of the speaker's own self or personal depth. The "expressive" model of language is different from the communication model. The communication model assumes that meaning inheres in the words themselves, while the expressivist model assumes that meaning resides in the speaker's inner emotional state. The expressivist model is more romantic than scientific, and is frequently used by those who wish to counter the communication model. The expressivist model is still quite widely held to be authoritative, alongside the communication model, and young preachers regularly claim that preaching is the preacher's self-expression. The womanist trajectory of the African American homiletical tradition is an exception, since many of the women theologians and homileticians assume that social values about male/female relationships are also conveyed.

While some measure of self-expression may indeed influence the use of language, it's probably simplistic to assume that self-expression is all that is happening. Even preachers who express their own emotions and inner states are not doing it ultimately for their own private catharsis, but to persuade others by their use of language. To put it bluntly, we use language to have influence over the thoughts and behaviors of others. Webb points out that such persuasion is not always overt, but sometimes extremely subtle. "Accepting a new viewpoint is not primarily a matter of someone's consciously 'changing one's mind'; instead, it is coaxing one, however indirectly, into modifying how one talks, into using the language that one wants the other to use...to talk differently is to align oneself in a different way."[52] Language is more than the

---

[51]Ivan Armstrong Richards, *The Philosophy of Rhetoric* (New York, London: Oxford University Press, 1936).

[52]Webb, *Old Texts, New Sermons,* 6.

speaker's self-expression; it is an act (intentional or not) that has influence over others.

Rhetorical studies and rhetorical critical studies consider language *in its use* to uncover the intending of written or oral discourse. Obviously, for me to say that the woman slit his gullet is an attempt to have you think in a certain way about the woman and her activities. Rhetorical studies continued to call into question the "science" of communication theory as well as of expressivist theories. Homileticians began to question whether it was more important to consider "how" words meant instead of "what" they meant. Again, the womanist theorists demonstrate more attention to rhetorical and rhetorical-critical issues than the male homileticians.

All these new understandings about language raised serious questions about the nature of truth, not only the "truth" of original meaning in a text, but the ways by which truth-claims themselves are sponsored by speakers and weighed by hearers. If language is as loaded and ambiguous as we have claimed, how could anything like absolute truth be borne in it? At best, Truth with a capital *T* is always partial and subject to human distortion. Language may have the ability to disclose some truth, but it probably always masks or hides some truth as well. We understand or approach truth through language, claims Gerhard Ebeling, and the study of language as an object will not disclose what we understand through language as an event. Ebeling and Ernst Fuchs, drawing on the work of Martin Heidegger and Rudolf Bultmann, argued that the event of speaking is what relates a text to a sermon, since human speech is an intersubjective event in which human meaning actually occurs through the negotiation of language.

Heidegger referred to language as "the house of being," by which we actually have any kind of world at all.[53] Meaning doesn't live in the past-tense world behind the text, but in the language itself, as it speak-happens into the human scene. Meaning "happens" through language. Truth "happens." Since language is ambiguous, and polyvalent, it's possible for it to mean different things at different times and in different speaking/hearing situations. Or as Paul Ricoeur has claimed, there is a surplus of meaning in any particular text or utterance. Meaning is not reduced to single words, to simple authorial intention, or even to the original rhetorical context itself. This trajectory is frequently called the

---

[53]Martin Heidegger, "Letter on Humanism," in his *Basic Writings: From Being and Time (1927) to The Task of Thinking (1964)* (New York: Harper & Row, 1977), 193.

New Hermeneutic, and it led in the 1970s and 1980s to the New Homiletic.[54]

The "revolution" in language studies has had a varied impact on homileticians. Some continue to operate as if the revolution never occurred, as it if is possible to master biblical languages and employ historical critical methods with enough precision to unlock something called "original meaning." Some of the homileticians we'll survey operate with implicit communication or expressivist models, some with keen insights into rhetorical studies, others with more sympathies for the New Hermeneutic.

---

[54]Paul J. Achtemeier, *An Introduction to the New Hermeneutic* (Philadelphia: Westminster Press, 1969); Robert W. Funk, *Language, Hermeneutic, and Word of God: The Problem of Language in the New Testament and Contemporary Theology* (New York: Harper & Row, 1966); James M. Robinson and John B. Cobb, eds., *The New Hermeneutic* (New York: Harper & Row, 1964); Gerhard Ebeling, *God and Word,* trans. James W. Leitch (Philadelphia: Fortress Press, 1967); Fred B. Craddock, *As One Without Authority: Essays on Inductive Preaching* (Enid, Okla.: Phillips University Press, 1971; 4th ed., St. Louis: Chalice Press, 2001); and David James Randolph, *The Renewal of Preaching* (Philadelphia: Fortress Press, 1969). David J. Lose, who teaches homiletics at Luther Seminary in St. Paul, Minnesota, has written an exceptional summary and analysis of the current state of the New Hermeneutic/New Homiletic. See his essay "Whither Hence, New Homiletic" (paper presented at the annual meeting of the Academy of Homiletics, Dallas , 2000), 255–66.

2

Samuel DeWitt Proctor

Samuel DeWitt Proctor was born in Norfolk, Virginia, in 1922; received his theological education at Crozer Theological Seminary and Yale Divinity School; and received his doctorate at The School of Theology at Boston University in 1950. Proctor served as pastor to Pond Street Baptist Church in Providence, Rhode Island, and then to Abyssinian Baptist Church in Harlem from 1972–1989, where he succeeded Adam Clayton Powell, Jr. He was also president of two colleges, Virginia Union University in Richmond (1955–1960), and North Carolina A & T State University (1960–1969). From 1969 to 1984, Proctor taught ethics at Rutgers University in New Brunswick, New Jersey, where he retired as Martin Luther King Professor, Emeritus. He served as associate director to the Peace Corps in Nigeria and Washington under Presidents Kennedy and Johnson, and held administrative positions with the National Council of Churches and the Office of Economic Opportunity.

Proctor lectured and preached all over the country, was a frequent baccalaureate speaker and guest lecturer, and held visiting professorships at Vanderbilt University Divinity School, United Theological Seminary, and Princeton Theological Seminary. He is the author of many books on religious faith and preaching, including *The Young Negro in America*, *Sermons from the Black Pulpit* (with William Watley), *Preaching about Crises in the Community, My Moral Odyssey, How Shall They Hear?, The Substance of Things Hoped For, The Certain Sound of the Trumpet,* and *We Have This Ministry: The Heart of the Pastor's Vocation* (with Gardner C. Taylor).

In 1997, Dr. Proctor was stricken with a heart attack as he talked with students after his lecture at Cornell College in Mount Vernon, Iowa. He died in a hospital in Cedar Rapids shortly thereafter.

Proctor is probably best characterized as being a social and religious moderate. His attention to the civil rights movement in the 1960s and to global justice and poverty issues was almost always tied to traditional issues of uplift, education, and moral character. His approach to faith was also that of a moderate Baptist preacher, tenderly cajoling people toward temperate discipleship. A contemporary of both Martin Luther King, Jr., and Malcolm X, he had little interest in either protest or aggression. He was a religious educator and social reformer in the mold of Booker T. Washington, an advocate of compromise, gradual change, and the value of education as a motivation for change.[1] His preaching method is grounded in this assumption, urging a Hegelian dialectic approach of thesis/antithesis/synthesis. Proctor's approach to sermon preparation was also indebted to Harry Emerson Fosdick's famous "project method," in which the preacher identifies a particular social or theological problem to be solved by the application of a biblical claim. Proctor claimed that one of the greatest tasks of the preacher was to instill Christian moral values through the careful articulation of New Testament principles, by which individuals would be nurtured toward greater faith.

Nature of the Gospel

The good news of Christian preaching is the assurance that God is with us in Jesus Christ. In the moral example of Jesus as teacher and example of a committed life, God has given us a great gift. "When we approach community concerns in the light of his life and teachings, there is a cleansing of the atmosphere, a steadying of our purpose, a correction in our course of action, a feeling of confidence that what we are doing is not whimsical or capricious and without foundation, but based upon the lasting and universal divine will."[2] The gospel is also good news about

---

[1]Proctor regularly mentioned Washington favorably in class comments and casual conversation.

[2]Samuel DeWitt Proctor, *Preaching about Crises in the Community* (Philadelphia: Westminster Press, 1988), 33.

the value of human life. Proctor claims that the gift of Jesus assures us that God esteems each and every human life. In this, Proctor's approach is similar to Martin Luther King's personalism, arguing for the dignity and worth of all persons, irrespective of status or birth. Jesus "put the worth of persons above the requirements of the law."[3] Our moral position, claims Proctor, derives from this fundamental understanding: Christians are called to affirm the worth of all persons and to renew our relationships with others. Faith is not a private matter, but is the foundation of our reconciling attempts for new beginnings and rehabilitation. Some situations may call for more than "one-to-one charitable responses" and may demand challenges to "institutional behavior that denies the worth of persons."[4] However, moral indignation must always be tempered by Christian love, patience, and humility. The good news illustrates the need for what Proctor calls "disciplined obedience." Christians don't have the choice between personal righteousness and service to others. Preachers proclaim the good news of God's affirming presence in Jesus Christ, and do so to bring about increased moral character in relationships and public life.

Relationship between Preaching and Scripture

Proctor is no fundamentalist or literalist with regard to the biblical witness. He chides those who put too much trust in the Bible, claiming that such trust is an error of human pride. Blind trust is also a mistake in that it denies the Bible's own understanding of itself as a human faith document. "The Bible," writes Proctor, "did not invent God, Christ, or the church…before there was a New Testament, Jesus had grown up in Nazareth, in Joseph's carpentry shop."[5] Proctor reminds us that our proof-texting and proving strategies would stun the writers of scripture. "The Bible was never intended to be used as a catalog of quick fixes for imponderable issues."[6]

However, the Bible is authoritative and foundational for preaching, since it discloses a particular kind of God, a particular kind of faithfulness,

---

[3]Proctor, *Preaching about Crises,* 35. King's personalism emerged from his theological anthropology formed by the African American church, and was given metaphysical grounding through the work of Boston personalists Peter Bertocci, Edgar S. Brightman, L. Harold DeWolf, and Walter Muelder. See Lewis V. Baldwin, Jr., *There Is a Balm in Gilead: The Cultural Roots of Martin Luther King, Jr.* (Minneapolis: Fortress Press, 1991), 118; John J. Ansbro, *Martin Luther King, Jr.: The Making of a Mind* (Maryknoll, N.Y.: Orbis Books, 1982).

[4]Proctor, *Preaching about Crises,* 38.

[5]Ibid., 45.

[6]Ibid.

and the power of faith language that inspires and nurtures believers. We turn to the Bible, not as an instruction manual, but as a revelation of God within real human drama. The scriptures deal with broad themes rather than specific questions–the themes of human struggle, evil in persons and institutions, and our own tendencies toward moral indifference. "What is found in the Bible is a self-disclosure of God, a revelation that breaks into history and into the lives of people in the context of their social arrangements."[7]

Proctor also assumes that the primary content of a sermon is the biblical witness. While his own method of thesis/antithesis/synthesis is an attempt to make faith meaningful to real lives, his constant resource for this is the written word of God. He does not turn to theological or traditional claims as resources for addressing the problems of contemporary believers; he turns to the Bible. In spite of his warnings that the Bible is not an instruction manual, his own method tends to treat the scriptures as answer books. To find God's approach to a particular question, we must become Bible-saturated and develop a "Bible-based consciousness."[8] Proctor's approach places the Bible, and particularly the teachings of Jesus, at the center of theological discernment, calling into question his own claims that God's disclosure is ongoing or that the witness of the Spirit blows through the contemporary church. He tends to place revelation in the past tense, and directs preachers to "turn to the Bible in coping with the issues before us" and to ratify our present-tense experiences of God in the pages of the book.

Relationship between the Testaments

Proctor tends to read the First Testament in terms of a prophecy/fulfillment paradigm. For him, the biblical faith is evolutionary, culminating in the ultimate revelation of Jesus Christ. He describes a sort of moral development of the faith, from "tribal deity" to "loving parent"; "from external moral demands to internal moral controls; from narrow ethnic tribalism to a genuine spiritual community"; from objectifying women, children, and servants to accepting them as persons; from "emphasis on the abundance of things to the attainment of the abundant life."[9] This proposition, that the Second Testament revelation about the nature and identity of Jesus Christ is ultimate, tends to

---

[7]Ibid., 47.
[8]Ibid., 50–51.
[9]Ibid., 48.

trivialize or subordinate the Hebrew scriptures. The witness of the First Testament becomes little more than prelude, setting the stage and the themes for the supreme disclosure in the Second Testament. Certainly the bias lingers in Proctor's own choice of language, describing the faith of Israel as ethnic and the faith of the church as universal.

Proctor struggles mightily to claim authority for the First Testament, but its authority is ultimately derivative; it's authoritative only insofar as it lays the foundation for Jesus. Proctor's own sermons and public addresses clearly don't support such a theological position of Christian superiority. He firmly believes that God loves all humans equally, regardless of race, class, gender, or national origin. The key is that Proctor assumes this universality is a characteristic of Christianity and not of biblical Judaism. He repeatedly construes the relationship between the two testaments from a law/gospel paradigm, hinting that the First Testament is oriented toward external works and rules while the Christian revelation concerns inner spirituality. His theological position regarding the nature of the two testaments maintains a fundamental privileging of the Christian revelation, a ghost of Marcion's categorical rejection of the First Testament.[10] Proctor doesn't oppose the two testaments sharply, but clearly favors the more "mature" theology of the Second Testament. Yes, the same God is revealed in both testaments, but the Second Testament, in Proctor's eyes, reveals it more accurately and conclusively.

Purpose of Preaching

Beyond the goal of opening up the scriptures, Proctor assumes that the primary purpose of preaching is to create a spiritual and moral conversion within hearers. His understanding is consistent with a traditional American evangelical assumption that ethical and moral activity are motivated by inner experience. "The ultimate moral control is from within."[11] He contrasts the First Testament with the Second Testament most dramatically with this assumption, claiming that the faith of Israel was predicated on rules and social constraints on behavior. He

---

[10]Preachers who want to avoid all forms of anti-Judaism or anti-Semitism may want to read more. See Ronald J. Allen and John C. Holbert, *Holy Root, Holy Branches: Christian Preaching from the Old Testament* (Nashville: Abingdon Press, 1995); Howard Clark Kee and Irvin J. Borowsky, *Removing Anti-Judaism from the Pulpit* (New York: Continuum, 1996); J. Alfred Smith, Jr., *New Treasures from the Old: A Guide to Preaching from the Old Testament* (Elgin, Ill. Progressive National Baptist, 1987), 17ff.

[11]Proctor, *Preaching about Crises,* 51.

interprets this difference from a theory of child development; we have rules until we mature to the point that moral restraint becomes internalized. Christian faith, as an internal affair, represents an improvement on the First Testament's reliance on codes of conduct and exacting rules. "This moral restraint moved from external to internal restraint: from the authority/fear relationship to the loving parent/obedient child relationship."[12]

Therefore, if a preacher hopes to effect social transformation, the best way to do so is to change people's hearts. "A changed society calls for changed persons."[13] When preachers proclaim the unconditional love of God in Christ, people are converted from their fear and works-righteousness toward genuine love and service. The grace we experience "equips us with a new ego, a new personhood, a new self," and it is this new self that acts graciously toward others.[14] This necessary conversion can come no other way, claims Proctor, than from within. Such a conversion experience generates behavior that is "more genuine, more sincere, more volitional" than an outward compliance to expectations and commands.[15]

Proctor outlines four fundamentals for preaching that speak to this central purpose. The preacher operates with four primary faith propositions that should, overall, guide homiletical practices. The first is the assumption that *God is supreme,* present and active in human affairs and in all of creation. Proctor comes close to upholding a traditional theism; without using the language of omnipotence or power, he still maintains that God is wholly other and does intervene in the affairs of the world. Second is his anthropological claim that *human beings can be transformed,* renewed, and born again. Not only is God acting in the world, but we can change in accordance with that activity. The ethical claim comes next, that as a result of such transformation we can live in the conviction that *genuine human community is possible.* Finally, the eschatological claim: *our daily lives have meaning beyond our finitude.* Eternity and immortality are not just for future enjoyment, but are already part of present experience. The future gives meaning to the present.[16]

---

[12]Ibid., 52.
[13]Ibid., 54.
[14]Ibid., 53.
[15]Ibid., 52.
[16]Samuel Proctor, *How Shall They Hear?: Effective Preaching for Vital Faith* (Valley Forge, Pa.: Judson Press, 1992), 16–17.

Nature and Purpose of Faith Communities

All homiletic theories involve some assumptions about the nature of the church and its vocation. Preachers don't regularly acknowledge it, but their presuppositions about the church's identity and purpose shape their own decisions about preaching. Since we've already noted that Proctor favors the teachings and example of Jesus, and that he taught Christian ethics for years, we might expect that his understanding of the church is related to its ethical mission.

Proctor's assumptions are implied in his earlier works, but they come to the fore in *We Have This Ministry: The Heart of the Pastor's Vocation,* co-authored with longtime friend and colleague Gardner C. Taylor. Here Proctor merges his evangelical theology with a strong social gospel, echoing centuries of African American Christianity. He insists that the goal of guiding people to God and proclaiming possibilities for a new personal identity does not conflict with the larger goal of enhancing human community. The preacher's work is always a *public* theology, done within a cultural and social context; therefore, the preacher must be informed about things such as politics, science, psychology, education, and sociology. We should, he claims, "portray the divine-human relationship in light of all available knowledge."[17] And since there is no ultimate disjunction between personal and public life, the church should not stop short of being involved in the larger world.

Proctor insists that churches should address the various needs of human beings, certainly with an eye toward their particular constituencies, but also looking beyond the congregation. He makes it clear that he doesn't mean just the spiritual or emotional needs of people but also their economic, educational, political, and social needs. Reflecting on the continued de facto religious segregation of American Christianity, Proctor points out that white churches fail to interest African Americans. By tailoring their ministries to the needs of their own folks, many white churches simply fail to consider what Proctor considers to be legitimate common needs within the black community. Accordingly, African American churches have become so identified with social and political struggle that white Christians may not feel part of the ministry. Proctor acknowledges this to be the reality, though he refuses to accept it as ultimately desirable.

---

[17]Samuel Proctor and Gardner C. Taylor with Gary V. Simpson, *We Have This Ministry: The Heart of the Pastor's Vocation* (Valley Forge, Pa.: Judson Press, 1996), 19.

The church, he argues, is united under one Christ and has one common vocation: to be the prophetic presence of Christ living in the world now.[18] A true human community is diminished by inequality, and the true church is diminished by division, a unity theme we will see again in James Earl Massey's work. All Christians, regardless of social location, should be in the business of working toward the goal of a diverse and ethical human society.

Preaching should extend beyond the concerns of personal salvation to include the concerns of a shared social life. Preaching should deal with real diversity, telling the truth, debunking stereotypes, advocating for the poor, and empowering the powerless. Proctor is a social moderate, advocating for gradual change through the channels of local politics, educational reform, and legal reform. He deplores contemporary penal practices and the shambles of public education, but still encourages congregations to avoid hostility and aggression in their encounters. "Black pastors have to be careful that they advocate for justice and fairness in such a way as to keep open the opportunity for friendly neighborhood fellowship."[19] Indiscriminate "blasting" shuts down intergroup relations and "violates the most distinctive of Christian tenets, to love one's enemy."[20]

In a similar vein, Proctor discusses the issue of racial or ethnic identity within congregations, asserting that there must be a balance between establishing pride in a specific heritage and the goal of diverse human community. He continues to merge Christianity with what he considers the best of American idealism, to include all its people in one fair and just society, a strategy we will see again in Gardner Taylor's work. Any ultimate pretense toward pride, whether ethnic, religious, or national, must be rejected. Manifest destiny, assumptions of predestination for success, a strong self-reliance (what he calls the American "can-do" ethos), and social Darwinism are all manifestations of human pride. Such attitudes of superiority take many popular forms, and the preacher must be prepared to unmask self-serving ideas regardless of their status as conventional wisdom. Proctor's claims about disclosure of evil and unmasking anticipate the work of James Forbes and the womanists.

Ultimately, claims Proctor, the church should imitate the teachings and acts of Jesus. We should be mindful of "the least, the lost, and the left-behind."[21] Proctor urges charity, but also assumes that congregations

---

[18]Ibid., 123.
[19]Ibid., 113–14.
[20]Ibid., 114.
[21]Ibid., 115.

must move beyond simple charity to be advocates for "the indigent elderly, the illiterate, the mentally ill, AIDS sufferers, unregistered migrants, and the rural poor."[22] For Proctor, preaching about God's presence in Jesus, about our hope for new personal identity, and about our confidence in God's future will move the church toward moral and ethical virtue. "The pastor must recognize that when the church is silent and the pastor's interest in these matters is muted and inarticulate, there is hardly any other advocacy that we can count on."[23]

Racial Orientation and African American Studies

Proctor makes few claims for any special status for African American studies or the centrality of black experience. One of his earliest works dealing with African American experience, *The Young Negro in America, 1960–1980,* was first published in 1966, before the watershed work of James Cone on black theology.[24] Proctor clearly had strong commitments to the African American community and took the history of slavery and segregation seriously. In *The Young Negro,* Proctor analyzes the social situation of black youth from the perspective of traditional democratic values of individual freedom and American diversity, which he sees as consistent with fundamental Christian egalitarian ethics.

However, since his writing is prior to the Black Theology movement, Proctor does not make theological connections by appealing to a theology of liberation, to the emancipatory figure of Jesus, or to a "preferential option" for the oppressed. Proctor combines the theological outlook of Howard Thurman (common humanity as a ground for human community) with the pragmatism of early twentieth-century black uplift themes (echoing both W. E. B. DuBois and Booker T. Washington) to produce a strategy for social change that values reconciliation and civic justice through the ordinary channels of education, local politics, and community service. He advocates for participation in established organizations such as the NAACP and the Urban League, since these organizations hold ongoing community accountability, unlike the student protest groups of the 1960s.

In *My Moral Odyssey,* published in 1989, Proctor takes issue with emerging Afrocentric claims and black theology. He laments what he

---

[22]Ibid., 116.

[23]Ibid., 123–24.

[24]Samuel D. Proctor, *The Young Negro in America, 1960–1980* (New York: Association Press, 1966). For Cone's early work, see James H. Cone, *Black Theology and Black Power* (New York: Seabury Press, 1969); and *A Black Theology of Liberation* (Philadelphia: Lippincott, 1970).

characterizes as the turn away from inclusion and equality. "It was a movement toward separatism and rejection of white society and culture entirely…A movement began to gain support that called for blacks to assert their identity, not with America, but with their African roots."[25] While Proctor affirms recognizing and celebrating black history, he draws the line at an adversarial or oppositional pattern. Always he looks for the synthesis, the reconciliation of opposing viewpoints. The kingdom of God, he claims, is a vision of "reconciliation and aggressive love, for seeking opportunities for mutual reassessment of belligerent positions…It was difficult for many of us to find a place in a movement that countenanced violence, bitterness, and intransigent ethnocentricity."[26] He urges pastors to create situations for interracial conversation and activities, and to proclaim such a vision from the pulpit.

With regard to the role of the black church and particularly for black preaching, Proctor argues that there is too much diversity within the tradition either historically or currently to make accurate generalizations. He says African American preaching demonstrates the same diversity as other forms of American Christianity and should not be characterized either by style of delivery or theological assumptions. He urges preachers to vary their topics and sermon forms and to shy away from emotionalism or entertainment. Some sermons should celebrate, some should teach, some should inspire, some should exhort. But all preaching should point to the vision of a common humanity operating in love and justice, what King called the "beloved community." Preaching doesn't stop with merely describing diversity, but "continues to show how such diversity can be brought into the harmonious pursuit of common goals, with justice, fairness, and freedom."[27] Preaching should always operate in the subjunctive, the "as if" of God's anticipated future, the "possibilities of refined and improved human relations."[28]

---

[25]Samuel Proctor, *My Moral Odyssey* (Valley Forge, Pa.: Judson Press, 1989), 114. Since none of the African American Christian leaders or theologians were calling for complete nationalism or separation, it's unclear to whom Proctor was reacting in this writing. King had suggested an interim strategy that might require temporary separation (in *Where Do We Go From Here: Chaos or Community?* [New York: Harper & Row, 1967]), and Cone never called for an absolute separation of the races. It seems likely that Proctor was reacting to non-Christian African American leaders or to Black Power youth movements.
[26]Proctor, *My Moral Odyssey*, 114.
[27]Samuel Proctor, *The Certain Sound of the Trumpet: Crafting a Sermon of Authority* (Valley Forge, Pa.: Judson Press, 1994), 15.
[28]Ibid.

Preaching and Language Studies

Proctor doesn't appeal to any particular language or literary theories. He doesn't discuss narrative studies or metaphor; neither does he make any philosophical claims about the nature of language and meaning. As many of the "gentlemen" preachers of his generation, he favors biblical expressions and metaphors, the use of standard (white) English, and clarity of thought. His own style is given more to straightforward expression and language in what Aristotle and Augustine called the "moderate" rhetorical style, suited for teaching or educating the human spirit.

This distinctive pulpit style probably reflects the theological and homiletical resources of Proctor's own theological education. During the 1940s and 1950s, seminaries and theological schools regularly taught rhetoric as part of the foundational curriculum, and the pulpit giants were the great British orators of the previous century. Proctor undoubtedly studied Broadus's classical text on sacred rhetoric, and Proctor recommends studying the great preachers of previous generations. His books regularly acknowledge the influence of white homileticians: George Buttrick, Paul Scherer, Harry Emerson Fosdick. However, there is very little attention to the use of language, poetics, or metaphor. Proctor's attitude toward the use of language could probably be best characterized as the "plain style" attributed to Puritan preachers.

Homiletic Method

Proctor's approach both to language and to underlying sermon structure owe much to Puritan plain style. As Ron Allen has described it, the plain style has the virtues of clarity and simplicity as it helps the congregation consider forthrightly how the gospel intersects with our world.[29] Plain-style preaching is given to propositional statements and an explication/application sermon form, regardless of the form of the text. Puritans adopted the plain style as an explicit alternative to the ornate preaching of their contemporaries. Plain-style preaching tends to circumvent ambiguity and subjectivity, opting for an objective "common sense" approach to interpretation and understanding.

---

[29]Ronald J. Allen, *Interpreting the Gospel: An Introduction to Preaching* (St. Louis: Chalice Press, 1998), 177–79.

Proctor's particular appropriation of the plain or propositional style is most informed by Hegel's pattern of "thesis-antithesis-synthesis" problem-solving. The ideal or sought-after situation is understood as the "thesis" proposition, that which is to be desired (liberation for the captives). The antithesis is the situation as it really is, less than ideal and fully grounded in the current historical context (more people are in prison than ever before in history). The solution is the synthesis, "which has come about from taking into account both the thesis and the antithesis. Neither one alone would have led to this particular solution."[30] The synthesis or solution comes about as a result of the "relevant question," which identifies the major obstacle to realizing the thesis. Proctor provides examples of relevant questions that should help the preacher identify and develop the significant body of the sermon. How did the family become so threatened? What is the real case for holding on to the nuclear family? If we lost the family, how serious would that be?

While Proctor suggests that this method is most suited for sermons dealing with community concerns, his own ethical mandates and his focus on the parables and teachings of Jesus suggest that preaching is most regularly a dealing in practical concerns and daily living. Proctor also explains how the thesis-antithesis-synthesis model works for dealing with doctrinal preaching, since it "approaches people where they *are* and delivers them to where they *ought to be.*"[31] Mervyn Warren has characterized Proctor's preaching as a "truth-style," which appeals mainly to the "middle class learning process" in its subdued pursuit of logic and prescription.[32] The style's clarity and relative emotional neutrality make it extremely popular at commencements, conferences, and university worship. Since Proctor's style was never polemical or confrontational, he found a wide hearing in middle- to upper-class white and African American audiences.

One of the greatest strengths of Proctor's theological approach is the way he matter-of-factly assumes that the parables and teachings of Jesus are for practical daily living. For Proctor, Christian faith is rugged and suited to the ordinary tasks of raising children, developing educational programs, making political decisions, solving neighborhood crime, and other humble chores. Christian faith is not some lofty philosophy, but a practical approach to understanding the human predicament that

---

[30]Proctor, *Preaching about Crises,* 118.

[31]Ibid., 127.

[32]Mervyn Warren, *Black Preaching: Truth and Soul* (Washington, D.C.: University Press of America, 1977), 34–36.

can inform just about every phase of domestic life. In this, Proctor definitely follows Harry Emerson Fosdick's "project method," by identifying an issue or problem that really does interest the ordinary believer and showing how a Christian understanding can shed light on the solution.[33] Proctor makes Christianity practical, direct, and down-to-earth.

His homiletic method, while predictable and perhaps unaesthetic, offers a solid and respectable approach that has served the church reliably for centuries. While most pastors will not want to use the plain style or the Hegelian method as standard fare, all pastors should be familiar with it. As Ron Allen reminds us, it has the advantage of clarity and directness. Where imagination or inspiration fails the preacher, this formula offers the option of contrast, proposition, and application. It is close to the people, close to the Bible, and has few distractions from the main proposal.

---

[33]Fosdick proposed a homiletic method grounded in ordinary human problems, particularly psychological problems. See Harry Emerson Fosdick, "Personal Counseling and Preaching," *Pastoral Psychology* (March 1952): 11–15.

3

Gardner Calvin Taylor

Gardner C. Taylor is considered by those inside and outside the African American preaching tradition to be one of the greatest preachers of the twentieth century. Taylor, a preacher's son, was born in 1918 and raised in Louisiana. He attended Leland College and Oberlin Graduate School of Theology. His first full-time pastorate (1941–1943) was in Ohio at Beulah Baptist Church. From 1943 to 1947, he served the congregation of Mt. Zion Baptist Church in Baton Rouge, where his father had preached several years before.[1] He assumed his most well-known pastorate at Brooklyn's Concord Baptist Church of Christ in 1948, a pastorate he held for forty-three years.

Taylor has lectured extensively and taught homiletics at Colgate Rochester Divinity School, Harvard Divinity School, and Union Theological Seminary. He has received honorary degrees from Benedict College, Leland College, and Albright College; and the Republic of Liberia has conferred on him Knight Commander, Order of African Redemption, and the Order of the Star of Africa. Primarily a preacher and pastor, he has published sermons in homiletical journals, two

---

[1] Gerald Lamont Thomas, "African American Preaching: The Contribution of Gardner C. Taylor" (Ph.D. diss., Southern Baptist Seminary, Louisville, Ky., 1993), 174–77.

sermon collections (*The Scarlet Thread* and *Chariots Aflame*), the occasional essay (chapter in Don M. Wardlaw, ed., *Preaching Biblically*), and the 1976 Lyman Beecher Lectures, published as *How Shall They Preach.*

Very little of the brief biographical material on Taylor mentions his participation in the civil rights movement of the 1960s or the fact that his social action candidacy in the National Baptist Convention split the denomination along liberal/conservative lines.[2] In 1960, Taylor was backed by Martin Luther King, Jr., to challenge the politically moderate incumbent Joseph H. Jackson, who had refused to endorse King's activities or to back the Southern Christian Leadership Conference. Taylor was elected in a riotous election, but Jackson refused to relinquish control of the treasury or any of the Convention property. Since the board of directors was still loyal to Jackson, attempts to oust him through the federal courts were futile.[3] The controversy led to the formation of the Progressive National Baptist Convention, of which Taylor was elected president a few years later (1967). Taylor was a mentor to Martin Luther King, Jr., assisting with a voter-registration plan that won the support of the African American churches. He was also a powerful member of the National Action Council of the Congress of Racial Equality (CORE), and was personally responsible for the CORE appointment of James Farmer, architect of the freedom rides.[4]

Taylor's personal history of social advocacy and civil rights activities is important to understand, because they established him in the African American Christian community (and to some extent within the white Christian community) as a pastor with prophetic concerns. His message may occasionally seem mild, but his person and his history, along with the history of the African Americans who hear him, radicalize the message in ways that white congregations may not recognize. He is a theological moderate, but a political progressive, and probably could be fairly characterized as somewhat more of an activist than Proctor.[5]

---

[2]Thomas's "African American Preaching" is a much-needed exception. Before his rhetorical analysis of several sermons, Thomas provides thorough biographical background gathered from Taylor and from Laura Scott Taylor, prior to her death in 1995.

[3]Taylor Branch, *Parting the Waters: America in the King Years 1954–1963* (New York: Simon & Schuster, 1988), 335–39.

[4]Ibid., 388–90.

[5]See Mervyn A. Warren's typologies of preaching styles in *Black Preaching: Truth and Soul* (Washington, D.C.: University Press of America, 1977). Warren's study actually has more to do with sermon content and rhetorical approaches than with delivery. See also Janice Denise Hamlet, "Religious Discourse as Cultural Narrative: A Critical Analysis of the Rhetoric of African-American Sermons" (Ph.D. diss., Ohio State University, 1989). Hamlet explores rhetorical strategies used by African American preachers during the civil rights era, and a sermon by Taylor is featured.

Taylor was, in fact, politically active for a period, but gave up active politics when he felt it was jeopardizing his ability to minister and preach effectively.

Nature of the Gospel

Taylor's Beecher lectures center on three themes: the nature of the gospel, the personality of the preacher, and the nature of the hearer. Taylor states quite bluntly that the gospel is a life-and-death matter and that trusting in the grace of God is the fundamental orientation to a life of justice and righteousness.

> If the undertaking does not have some sanctions beyond human reckoning, then it is indeed rash and audacious for one person to dare to stand up before or among other people and declare that he or she brings from the Eternal God a message for those who listen that involves issues nothing less than those of life and death.[6]

Taylor's intention is to create an experience of faith through preaching, not merely to discuss faith or to discuss the gospel. Preaching should embody faith, not just talk about faith according to the demands of historical, exegetical, or scientific methods. Preaching goes beyond an account of past-tense events to create within the congregation a present-tense experience of grace. "The preacher ought to try," claims Taylor, "to bring the people before the presence of God and within sight of the heart of Christ."[7]

Taylor's assumptions about presence require explicit attention. He assumes that the God we know in Jesus the Christ is present in the activity of preaching. The preacher's job is to point to this presence, to bring attention to the invisible immediacy of God with the people. In terms of language and poetics, the preacher invokes or names God. In terms of faith claims, the preacher speaks of a living Christ, a resurrected Savior, a risen Lord. Bluntly, the gospel claims that in the presence of the risen Christ, God's grace is made manifest here and now. Preaching names the dead as present, making a predecessor vividly present to congregational imagination as alive and active. Taylor uses the present

---

[6]Gardner C. Taylor, *How Shall They Preach* (Elgin, Ill.: Progressive Baptist Publishing House, 1977), 24.

[7]Gardner C. Taylor, "Shaping Sermons by the Shape of Text and Preacher," in *Preaching Biblically*, ed. Don M. Wardlaw (Philadelphia: Westminster, 1983), 142.

tense carefully, bringing the congregation into the presence of God and within the sight of Christ. This is, in fact, the polar opposite of escapism. Believers cannot escape the homiletic presence of a living God who tramps up and down the aisles, who groans and weeps in their midst, who carts out the dinnerware and throws a party and who gestures with a nail-torn palm for them to follow.

The personality of the preacher and the personality of the hearers are corollaries of these claims about the gospel and its language. While Taylor has high expectations of the pastoral office, he seems to mean something slightly different from assumptions that the preacher must be likeable and praiseworthy. When Taylor speaks of personality, whether of the preacher or of the hearers, he seems to be making a claim about theological anthropology and what it means to recognize and take seriously the whole predicament of being human.

> The magnificent anomaly of preaching is to be found in the fact that the person who preaches is in need himself or herself of the message which the preacher believes he or she is ordained to utter...what is wrong with the hearers is the same thing that is the matter with the preacher...a guilty one telling guilty ones of the judgment upon them and a mercy wider and kinder than the judgment, and more devastating.[8]

Purpose of Preaching

Preachers are to preach "the whole counsel of God" says Taylor, to be "watchmen" for the Lord, to interpret God to human beings. The watchtower/sentry model developed in the Beecher lectures allows him to develop a double homiletic purpose. First, the preacher must be devoted to vigilant watching for any signs of trouble, whether it be a spiritual enemy or a more social and political enemy that "lurks on the far edges of the horizon where the sky seems to meet the earth."[9] The preacher as sentry does not direct his or her gaze primarily at the people or at the compound, but toward the world surrounding the community. The sentry is not allowed to claim indifference or fatigue, having been appointed by the community for this critical task, and it would be better for the people to have no sentry at all than to "be lulled into a false security by the notion that a qualified watchman stands to

---

[8]Taylor, *How Shall They Preach*, 27, 29, 30.
[9]Ibid., 79.

the job, when in fact, the watchman cannot see, or is asleep, or has been influenced by other considerations to close the eyes and turn the back to any hazard which may be gathering in the distance."[10]

Second, the preacher as sentry must sound the alarm and warn the community when trouble is on the horizon. Taylor is not suggesting that all problems come from the outside, but obviously suggests that the preacher is appointed to do more than see and take notice; the preacher is obligated to announce the problem to the community under threat. "There is little place for ranting by the preacher, but there is a very large place, indeed, for urgency and for an earnest, honest passion. The stakes are high! The watchman is involved; the community under threat is his or her community."[11]

Taylor doesn't advocate taking explicitly political positions, but claims that preachers must consider political issues to be subject to theological reflection.[12] He considers the most routine social and political issues to be fundamentally theological, yet the popular discussions about them are all too often grounded in faulty assumptions about what it means to be human and what is worthy of ultimate loyalty. "At any rate, the preacher has no warrant to speak to our social ills save in the light of God's judgment and God's grace."[13]

Language Studies and Preaching

All this underscores how critical language is for Taylor. He does not consider language to be a mere ornamentation, but rather that poetic language is the essential currency of ideas and understanding.[14] In this regard, Taylor likens preaching to literature or theater, which uses language to plumb the "deeper matters of human life in ways we preachers seem often afraid to confront."[15] The love of language and an appreciation for its mystery are at the convergence of Taylor's tradition and formal education. The slave preachers and storytellers, the griots of tribal Africa, have the same passion for using the language that great contemporary preachers have. He mentions particularly the

---

[10]Ibid.

[11]Ibid., 80.

[12]Samuel Proctor and Gardner C. Taylor with Gary V. Simpson, *We Have This Ministry: The Heart of the Pastor's Vocation* (Valley Forge, Pa.: Judson Press, 1996), 127–28.

[13]Taylor, *How Shall They Preach*, 84.

[14]Gardner C. Taylor, "The Sweet Torture of Sunday Morning," *Leadership* (Summer 1981): 28.

[15]Michael Duduit, "Preaching and the Power of Words: An Interview with Gardner C. Taylor," *Preaching* (January-February 1994): 3.

love of metaphor, which he grew to appreciate under the tutelage of Paul Scherer. Preaching, as an oral activity, depends on the vivid potentiality or promise of language for carrying its truth. Taylor refers to this animism of language as contributing a kind of apocalyptic quality to thinking, a gift for indirect statement, an awareness of mysterious otherness, and a sense that time is mysteriously telescoped. Walter Ong writes about the same understanding, claiming that the primacy of sound presents a God who is personal, who is beyond us but deeply present to our inner selves, like the sound of voice. The word is an event in history that emerges and perishes in time, maintained only as oral event in memory. The word is not a record that is static and accessible to any individual, but a dynamic presence in the communal memory that keeps the significant past alive in the present.[16]

Taylor also understands the performative nature of language. When asked in an interview about keys to audience understanding, Taylor responded immediately that language is one of the most critical factors. He qualified his answer by indicating the distinction between what language does and how it carries out its work, making the same suggestion that rhetoricians make: that content and form are necessarily related. Word choice is not just a matter of definition, but of mode or manner. "Words must make definite suggestions, not only in their definition but in their sound. There are words that caress, words that lash and cut, words that lift, and words that have a glow in them."[17] We need to notice that Taylor is not talking about the style of delivery, but the style of the words and phrases themselves. Taylor even paraphrases T. S. Eliot by referring to preaching as "a raid on the inarticulate and inexpressible."[18]

This understanding of language as an oral event, as having both immediacy and transcendence, as participating incarnationally in its own purpose, allows Taylor to connect preaching and the gospel theologically. At the same time that proclamation has life and power, it is also weak: preaching is humbled, dependent on something fleeting and frail; oral language begins to perish as soon as it is uttered. Language and the gospel are both subject to temporality, fragility, and futility. Taylor speculates that he could have come up with a better way to transmit the gospel than the insubstantial weakness of language. Words may have power,

---

[16]Walter J. Ong, *The Presence of the Word* (New Haven, Conn.: Yale University Press, 1967).
[17]Duduit, "Preaching and the Power of Words," 3.
[18]Taylor, "Sweet Torture," 27. Taylor refers to Eliot's poem, "East Coker."

but they have a finite and ephemeral power. Words perish. "How strange of God to make the uttered word, so fragile and so tenuous, the principal carrier of so precious a cargo."[19]

Nature and Purpose of Faith Communities

The gospel spoken in preaching constitutes a community of believers who can transcend their individuality and be bound together by a larger vision:

> It says to those ages which deify the individual, the personal, that we are all of one blood, members of the family of man, all bound in the bundle of life.[20]

So constituted, the community of believers is corporately committed to ethical activity within the sociohistorical realm. Spirituality and ethical behavior are but different dimensions of the religious truth of the gospel.

> The great corporate issues of our society—poverty, pollution, the international violence of war, anarchy, race and the national priorities—are not primarily political matters; they are rooted profoundly in our attitude toward the God whose retainer the preacher is honored to be.[21]

Preaching includes critique. Taylor has great respect for American democratic ideals and, like Martin Luther King, Jr., and Samuel Proctor, considers that the gospel vision and the American dream can enhance each other, offering a purposeful synthesis of civil and religious ideals. He frequently quotes from the Constitution and from the Declaration of Independence to orient hearers to a foundational vision of sociopolitical life.

He has not abandoned hope for racial harmony, and assumes that the United States "has an ordination in history," along with other nations, to work toward a vision of justice. He is clear, though, that this is not an election, or a pure manifest destiny. The country is not exempt from religious critique. This puts Taylor in the theological category that might be called progressive millennialism, embracing Christianity and

---

[19]Taylor, *How Shall They Preach,* 44.
[20]Ibid., 92.
[21]Ibid., 83.

the role of the church in a prophetic stance toward American culture.[22] In one sermon, he critiques America's failure to honor its national vision, aligning it with religious despair.

> Hopefulness sometimes seems gone from the nation as we settle into predictably ruinous patterns of greed and selfishness, with no sense of grand adventure in human betterment and making this truly "a more perfect union."[23]

He is quick to distinguish his own understandings from the reduction of Christianity to civil religion, and demands that the preacher have "some impossible place" to stand to identify nationalism as idolatry and civil religion as "an enslavement to the culture."[24] The gospel ends up being a critique of earthly power that "points out how fragile all our human situations are...to point to all this power and the structures that enslave us and to say, 'It has no power.'"[25]

The vocation of the church derives from an eschatological understanding of God's hope for the whole human community. The church is that prophetic community that continues to manifest mercy and justice in its own corporate life and to call for mercy and justice in the broader social sphere. The church offers a social vision of human relationships, transformed by its own appropriation of mercy. Where Proctor's unit of moral value is the human individual, transformed and committed, Taylor's leans more toward the corporate: our vocation is to be a certain kind of community rather than just certain kinds of individuals.

This eschatological vocation surfaces in Taylor's own illustrations and images, where lonely individuals are reunited with a blessed community of the future. Taylor's sermons frequently feature enormous imaginative crowd scenes, full of angels, saints, ordinary believers, and unknown decendents. He doesn't preach in a literal apocalyptic mode, predicting times and places, but uses eschatological and apocalyptic visions of community to critique the historical present.

---

[22]This characterization of progressive millennialism is Timothy E. Fulop's. See his essay "The Future Golden Day of the Race: Millennialism and Black Americans in the Nadir, 1877-1901," in *African-American Religion: Interpretive Essays in History and Culture*, ed. Timothy E. Fulop and Albert J. Raboteau (New York: Routledge, 1997), 231.

[23]Gardner C. Taylor, "The Easter Victory," *Pulpit Digest* (March/April 1990): 31.

[24]Gardner C. Taylor, interview by author, October 1995.

[25]Ibid.

Although he believes that apocalyptic eschatology reveals something about the nature of God's intentions for the future, that future should never lose its relationship to the present situation. Commenting on the apocalyptic rhetoric of the civil rights era, he claims that nobody "in a minority situation, certainly given our racial situation in America, could avoid some apocalyptic emphasis."[26] While Taylor thinks that both Martin Luther King, Jr., and Malcolm X were forced to use such dramatic language because the situation was so desperate, he bemoans the loss of the apocalyptic perspective today. "I think that younger preachers are still suffering the backlash from that otherworldly thing."[27] The otherworldly vision has a power of critique, and its loss has resulted in a kind of social anomie.

> I think that the African American community is heading for very uncertain times. For the first time in my life, as I see it, nobody seems to know what the next step ought to be. We were often wrong, but we were all convinced that we knew what was next, and what ought to be, and how we'd try to reach it. I'm not sure that exists today... [apocalyptic] certainly can be the enemy. But I think the history of our struggle will indicate that it was not the enemy of change. Whatever change came, came partly through that kind of vision.[28]

While Taylor embraces a prophetic stance toward contemporary culture, he's still reluctant to advocate for congregations to operate in the full activist mode. Part of his concern seems to be his understanding of the church itself as a community that lives between worlds and is not fully identified by its secular context. Another part of his concern has to do with the abuse of leadership roles, the dangers of pastoral arrogance, and the diversity within the congregation. "Whether or not the pastor participates in partisan politics, the congregation expects him or her to be able to identify the failures and needs in government and politics...but the pastor should think carefully about using biblical criteria and paradigms to make his or her political agenda clear."[29] He cautions against what he calls "political moralizing" and what Walter Brueggemann characterizes as a limited prophetic perspective.

---

[26]Ibid.
[27]Ibid.
[28]Ibid.
[29]Proctor and Taylor, *We Have This Ministry*, 127–28.

Brueggemann claims that the more prophetic activity is to continue to hold before the people an alternative vision of human community by which to critique; he rejects the position where Christian vocation is an "ad hoc liberalism," reducing prophecy to righteous indignation over present crises.[30] This seems to be Taylor's position as well, since he continues to press for a vision of the future that critiques but does not reduce theology to liberal politics.

Taylor doesn't reject the idea of political action, or even of elected public office for the pastor. Nonetheless, he cautions pastors to examine their own motives as well as the presence of other qualified candidates. While a sociopolitical paradigm for ministry is not categorically ruled out, neither is it the primary vocational agenda for the pastor or the congregation. Taylor's understanding of community vocation is similar to Proctor's civic model, but with greater possibilities in the direction of the activist model.

Mervyn Warren has characterized Taylor as a "methods" preacher, distinct from the "ethics" preachers such as Jesse Jackson, James Cone, Albert Cleage, and so forth. The force of an ethics-style preacher derives more from the moral authority of a prophetic position than from the homiletic presentation itself. Warren claims that the methods style demands analysis along with a persuasive presentation of that analysis. Preaching as persuasion is critical to the methods style and operates more effectively in congregations of mixed sociopolitical commitments.

Relationship between Preaching and Scripture

Taylor has a deep respect for the biblical witness, claiming that it is both eternal and relevant, and even cites Barth's observation that the preacher should preach with the Bible in one hand and the newspaper in the other.[31] However, while Taylor does frequently preach "on a text," he rarely deals with a portion of text as a world unto itself, and certainly never claims that Christian preaching must always deal with the Bible. Rather, the scriptures are a resource for the ongoing discernment of the good news, "the tender love call of the Everlasting God aimed at His erring and straying creation."[32] The scriptures, studied properly, become a living witness to the living God. The main thrust of the

---

[30]Walter Brueggemann, *The Prophetic Imagination* (Minneapolis: Fortress Press, 1978), 11–15.
[31]Taylor, *How Shall They Preach,* 62. See the discussion of Barth's comments in chapter 1.
[32]Ibid., 60.

biblical witness is that God reaches out to a dearly beloved world, luring, always luring chaos into a loving relationship. We human creatures are restless, and God is restless, always yearning for reunion. "What of that Word which became flesh at Bethlehem and in Nazareth and Galilee and Jerusalem, at Calvary and in a cemetery addressing itself to the formless, the void, the darkness in every human creature and in every age?"[33]

If the preacher understands the scripture rightly, preaching from the Bible will address the great existential themes of human meaning: hope, despair, fear, trust, loyalty, courage. Taylor is perhaps the most existential of the contemporary black homileticians, following Bultmann's hermeneutical approach to make claims about meaning in the face of human meaninglessness. And for this task many of the great classics are as generative as the Bible. Taylor advises preachers to study great music and literature, historic documents, poetry, drama. "Sermons are everywhere, for the critical encounter between God and his creation, and particularly his supreme creation, human kind, is forever occurring, world without end."[34] He is as apt to preach insights from the Declaration of Independence as from Shakespeare, since the preacher must always speak to the deepest doubts, longings, and weaknesses of the human heart. In this sense, the pages of scripture are our own peculiar version of the classic quest for comfort, joy, and meaning. Truth is not, however, confined to the church's canonical texts. God, as a living being, emerges in the deep encounters elicited by text, nature, music, art, poetry, a glance. The Word, he reminds us, became flesh and dwelt among us. Whether we preach from the Bible or from some other source, the preacher is called to declare an abiding love that meets deep human loneliness.

The Bible, then, is not an answer book for those seeking to know which behaviors are right and wrong, or to find solutions for problems. Taylor, unlike Proctor, rarely preaches from the teachings of Jesus. He finds in the Bible an answer to existential rather than moral questions, not how to do this or how to do that, less attention to becoming more Christlike behaviorally than to becoming Christlike existentially. The Bible is best understood philosophically as that witness to deep meaning. In this regard, scripture is less imperative and more indicative, disclosing the truth of how God *is* in relationship to the world.

---

[33]Ibid., 61.
[34]Ibid.

Relationship between the Testaments

One of Taylor's sermon titles ultimately became the title for the whole collection. This phrase, "the scarlet thread," refers to what Taylor considers to be the grand theological theme uniting both testaments. "God is out to get back what belongs to him."[35] The preacher who has a good grasp of the full sweep of scripture will discover the divine longing and will articulate the same truth whether preaching from the Hebrew Bible or the New Testament. This certainly doesn't mean that every sermon will boil down to this propositional claim, but it does mean that this theological foundation informs all subsequent claims. In light of this unshakable belief, the preacher will explore, through different characters and narratives, all the dimensions of our distance from God and God's desire for reunion. Nobody has to work hard to make the scriptures relevant, claims Taylor; they already are. "The preacher only has to communicate the relevance that is native to the theme. The Bible is full of life-and-blood people: it's frightfully honest."[36]

On christocentrism: "The Christian preacher must not strain to make the Christ event explicit in every sermon. Where it is at all reasonable to state it, one ought."[37] In a sermon for Good Friday, Taylor sets forth a traditional Anselmian sustitutionary atonement theory, but stops short of claiming that the Hebrew Bible is mere prophecy that Christ fulfills. Taylor's understanding of the relationship between the testaments is more continuous. He cites Psalm 72, "of one who shall deliver the needy and redeem their souls"; he cites Isaiah's prophetic hope for "a warrior with garments rolled in blood"; he cites Zechariah's "fountain opened in the house of David." Then, without missing a beat, Taylor muses, "Not clear and conscious prophecies of Christ, I think, but conclusions from gazing in the direction of the everlasting God."[38]

Preaching and Liturgy

Nothing in Taylor's writing indicates a relationship between preaching and liturgical or sacramental practices. His comments about making the living God in Christ present, and his homiletical appropriation of Anselmian substitutionary atonement would be the most likely connections. Standard Baptist practices of the Lord's supper tend more

---

[35]Taylor, "Sweet Torture," 20.
[36]Ibid.
[37]Taylor, "Shaping Sermons," 151.
[38]Taylor, *How Shall They Preach,* 145.

toward a remembrance or a memorial observation than a "making present" of the risen Christ, however. There is enough ambiguity in Taylor's own understanding of the relationship between atonement and resurrection to make any sacramental or liturgical connections difficult to predict.

Homiletic Method

The Beecher lectures reveal very little about Taylor's methodological strategies. Taylor provides some general philosophical guidelines about the nature of the preacher, the nature of human experience, and the necessity for the preacher to be sensitive and poetic, but he does not offer much in terms of technique. We never have a chance to see Taylor in action. We never see his exegetical approach, his determination of sermon structure, or how he selects illustrations, images, or words.

His chapter in the Wardlaw collection offers little more insight. Taylor claims that the shape of text and preacher interact; particular images or narrative styles will be more suited to a preacher's peculiar style. His discussion of the preacher's style has little to do with delivery, but with the way of developing a sermon as logical, intuitive, expansive, dialectical, or prophetic.

However, he says the preacher will allow the shape and flow of the text to control the flow and logic of the sermon.[39] He recognizes that texts, as recorded rhetorical or narrative bits, all have rhetorical or narrative intentions. The texts, like other persuasive conversation, intend to create some type of particular understanding, action, or decision within the hearers. Exegesis or other scholarly study should not focus primarily on the details of a text, but should assist in understanding the overall purpose and intention of the selection.

To this end, the whole narrative sweep of the passage or chapter may provide clues to understanding, and Taylor urges preachers to "walk up and down the street on which a text lives. The surrounding terrain ought to be taken into account."[40] This has less to do with the historical context of the author and more to do with the integrity of the text as a rhetorical and narrative whole. Taylor wants us to ask what is at stake in a particular text and its theological claims, and not to waste time poking around where there is little theological reward. Preaching should not deal with trivialities; preaching is neither "trivial nor fancy nor syrupy

---

[39]Taylor, "Shaping Sermons," 138–41.
[40]Ibid., 139.

nor mean nor truckling to any human pride or pretense." It ought to be a word "as from a dying person to dying people," and to "do business in the supreme matters of human life."[41]

The most helpful clues to sermon preparation lie in Taylor's own theological assumptions. First, his existentialist leanings suggest that one of the fundamental human dramas is the quest for meaning. Religious meaning, whether for the individual or for the community, resides in reunion with God and with that which lies "beyond the veil of mortality." Death, loneliness, fear of death, fear of loneliness: these are the terrors of being human. Happily, we find meaning in human/human reunion and in human/divine reunion. Taylor's theological anthropology, stated in classical terms as estrangement or exile, is key to his homiletic method.

If theological anthropology is central, so is the nature of God's own character and project. God is no less lonely or estranged than we are, and God yearns for the same reunion we crave. "God is out to get back what belongs to him." This is why Taylor works so hard in his sermons to create that sense of immediacy and presence, using the present tense, speaking anthropomorphically of God, making the language bear the presence of divinity. Taylor is convinced that we are lonely for God and need to experience God's presence. "The preacher ought to try to bring the people before the presence of God and within sight of the heart of Christ. No sermon can do more. None should want to do less."[42]

Taylor's homiletical strategy is to articulate our alienation and to name it theologically. His sermons frequently begin with that cool introduction, forging a kind of psychological common ground wherein the listeners all identify with some common human experience. We are uncertain, afraid, uneasy, apprehensive, anxious. Taylor then moves on to draw out the implications of our situation and to speculate about solutions or desires for resolution. At some point in the sermon, Taylor will usually paint a parallel portrait of God's own dissatisfaction with the current state of affairs and God's desire for reconciliation. The sermon moves from estrangement to reconciliation, reunion, and restoration. Sometimes Taylor takes us just to the edge of reunion or full restoration, leaving the veil intact but slightly opaque. There is a

[41]Ibid., 143.
[42]Ibid., 142.

mythic pattern of the heroic quest, but the quest reunites the individual with his or her community, usually just short of the promised land.

Taylor's existentialism and his understanding of language to evoke presence put him more squarely in the New Hermeneutic/Homiletic than any of the others we survey. Taylor doesn't discuss language theory in any depth, but his is more thoroughly formed by the New Hermeneutic than either Massey or Mitchell, who *do* refer to the New Homiletic.

Taylor's rhetorical style varies within each sermon, depending on the idea or strategy he uses. He is capable of the grand and inspirational style, and is usually remembered most for his sweeping and poetic high oratory. When he operates in the inspirational mode, he selects inspirational illustrations, frequently drawn from Western classics (the arts, literature, music, speeches), from American historical patriotic documents, and from other inspirational biblical images. However, his sermons regularly feature a more subdued and reflective rhetorical style alongside a moderate and commonsense approach, and his word choice and illustrative material change appropriately, using examples from science or ordinary life. He is exceptionally good at describing or recreating the processes of human thought and the phenomenology of ordinary experience. "When we were young, our teeth seemed so unchangeably strong, our step so unalterably firm, our eyesight so permanently clear...all of this can pass so quickly that we are left dazed as to where the beauty of our faces and the strength of our self-sufficiency went."[43]

Taylor's theology and his homiletic method frequently imitate a Pauline understanding of the faith struggle, Pauline reflections on that struggle, and Pauline rhetorical strategies (persuasion, confrontation, pleading, exhortation). Perhaps one of the greatest gifts of Taylor's preaching is the way it forces listeners to confront their own beliefs and thoughts. With Taylor, we reflect, remember, anticipate, yearn. His ability to turn a phrase, use onomatopoeia, work a metaphor, and hold a vision aloft in the palm of his hand works deeply, not so much on the emotions as on the imagination.

---

[43]Gardner Taylor, "Beauty Which Fadeth Not Away," in *Chariots Aflame* (Nashville: Broadman Press, 1988), 43.

4

James Earl Massey

James Earl Massey is dean, emeritus, at Anderson University School of Theology, the theological seminary of the Church of God (Anderson, Ind.). Dr. Massey also served for six years as dean of the chapel and professor of religion and society at Tuskegee University. For almost twenty years he was the senior minister of Metropolitan Church of God, a large multicultural congregation in Detroit.

Massey is the son and grandson of preachers and has three elder brothers who are also preachers. Massey recounts his own call to preaching at the age of sixteen, in Detroit, Michigan.[1] He was listening to a recording of Chopin preludes, carried away by the music, when he heard a voice compelling him to "go preach." Massey had been training to be a pianist in the European classical tradition, and his musical interests resurface in his approach to homiletic design.

He attended the Detroit Bible College (later named William Tyndale College), concentrating in Bible, theology, and biblical languages. He

---

[1]Barry L. Callen, ed., *Sharing Heaven's Music: The Heart of Christian Preaching, Essays in Honor of James Earl Massey* (Nashville: Abingdon Press, 1995, 203–4), an interview with Henry M. Mitchell. The Mitchell interview notes that Massey's call story, "Called While Reading a Score of Chopin," is recorded in *The Irresistible Urge to Preach: A Collection of African American "Call" Stories,* ed. William H. Myers (Atlanta: Aaron Press, 1992), 230–32. Another description of his call can be found in Massey's *The Burdensome Joy of Preaching* (Nashville: Abingdon Press, 1998), 29–30.

picked up some Greek classes at Wheaton College Graduate School after graduating from college, and then enrolled in seminary at Oberlin Graduate School of Theology. In addition to training in Bible and theology, he devoted his studies to speech and communication. When he was in the pastorate, he pursued postgraduate courses in communication arts at the University of Michigan.[2]

Massey grew up in what he claims was a bicultural Christian setting, since his local Church of God (Anderson) congregation was interracial, while the "Mother Church" in downtown Detroit was predominantly African American. The whole Church of God (Anderson) is predominantly white. "The congregation that met in our community was still interracial, however, and it was a rather intimate circle of members. I grew up in its life as one who sensed a God-given tie with all the other members, black and white. Belonging to that fellowship helped me to understand the meaning and application of the unity theme that was so often treated from the pulpit."[3]

Massey also notes other influences on his understanding of preaching that reflect a similar inclusivity. His father, George W. Massey, Sr., impressed him with his biblical knowledge and memorization skills; Raymond Jackson, the pastor who offered support to Massey during his teen years, taught him courage in the pulpit; Howard Thurman, whom Massey met in 1949 during his college years, impressed him with his spiritual depth; and George A. Buttrick, the white preacher, impressed him with his skills in sermon development and "provocative handling of a text."[4]

Massey was campus minister and assistant professor of religious studies at Anderson College in Indiana from 1969 to 1977. The General Assembly of the Church of God elected him Christian Brotherhood Hour speaker in 1977, and he held this post until 1982, when he was invited to be professor of New Testament and preaching at the Anderson School of Theology. He was the dean of the chapel and professor of religion at Tuskegee University between 1984 and 1989, and returned to Anderson School of Theology in 1989.[5]

---

[2]Callen, *Sharing Heaven's Music*, 205. I have found no record of an earned doctorate, either a Doctor of Ministry or a Doctor of Philosophy degree. Massey holds several honorary doctorates.

[3]Ibid., 206. The unity theme may be similar to reconciliation themes of the earlier civil rights era and is similar to Proctor's use of unity and reconciliation themes.

[4]Ibid., 205–6.

[5]Massey notes that he served the last seven years of his pastorate concurrently with the campus ministry duties. When he left Metropolitan Church of God in Detroit, he began the radio ministry at Anderson, according to Callen, *Sharing Heaven's Music*, 209.

Massey is an ordained minister in the Church of God (Anderson), and the author of numerous books and articles. Massey serves on several editorial boards, among them: *Preaching* magazine, *Leadership* magazine, *Best Sermons* (new series), and *Christianity Today.* He also is a contributing writer and editor for the twelve-volume *New Interpreter's Bible* and is widely sought for preaching and lectures on preaching.

Among his homiletical works are *The Responsible Pulpit, The Sermon in Perspective, Designing the Sermon,* and *The Burdensome Joy of Preaching.* He has coedited a book on homiletic theory (with Wayne McCown), *Interpreting God's Word For Today: An Inquiry into Hermeneutics From A Biblical Theological Perspective,* and there is a festschrift in his honor, *Sharing Heaven's Music: The Heart of Christian Preaching,* edited by Barry L. Callen.

Massey is probably best characterized as a theological and social conservative. When he refers to himself as a "radical" preacher, he means to suggest the radicality of cutting down to the root of preaching, which is the gospel's personal confrontation to each hearer. His commitment to Christian unity and human unity has likewise led him to avoid oppositional preaching that might create animosities between groups of people. His published sermons do not demonstrate significant prophetic critique, even though he claims that social critique is a necessary part of a black preacher's sermonic witness.

Nature of the Gospel

Massey's homiletic theory is summed up in a simple phrase: "Preach the gospel and work for justice." We'll consider some of the implications of social location and the American context later in the chapter, but for now, let's note that Massey considers the gospel to be necessarily linked to issues of social ethics. "Like every Christ-commissioned preacher, the black Christian preacher has had to preach the gospel, but he has also had to work actively against the social forces that undermine human dignity and make the gospel seem only a wealth of words."[6] Preaching is to be grace-centered, bearing the apostolic message of Jesus Christ as the unique Son of God. Massey specifically rejects the idea that Jesus is somehow simply re-presenting the truth about God, or that he's a moral exemplar, or that he is possessed of heightened spirituality or a developed sense of radical obedience. For Massey, the heart of the good news is first and foremost that Jesus Christ is truly "the godly son of one Joseph and Mary."[7]

---

[6]James Earl Massey, *The Responsible Pulpit* (Anderson, Ind.: Warner Press, 1974), 43.
[7]Ibid., 20.

Second, the gospel must be centered on "Christ crucified," which reveals that Christ died for us as a sacrifice on our behalf. The cross, rightly preached, reveals God's love for us as well as our own captivity to sin. "The word of the cross…is part of a larger, longer story and divine plan. It is redemptive because it assigns our sins to *his* volunteered and vicarious sacrifice. It is ruling because of the constraint its meaning makes upon our spirits."[8] The meaning of the cross is constant: an indictment of human sin, a witness to Christ's obedience, a gift of God's saving plan, and the atoning center of preaching. For Massey, the entire New Testament is commentary on the cross.[9]

In addition to the saving message of the cross, the gospel must also include the claim of resurrection. When Massey argues for preaching the cross and the resurrection, he does not deny the possibility that these will be troublesome or even incredible to his hearers. However, the resurrection is part of the apostolic message contained in the New Testament, and preachers must "affirm [it] as an event that is fixed in history, holding promise and potency of eternal dimensions."[10] Massey's discussion of the meaning of resurrection is only minimally developed, especially in contrast to his discussion of the meaning of the crucifixion. The primary mandate for preaching the resurrection is that it is part of the apostolic witness and something that the early church believed in. The fact that it seems incredible should humble contemporary Christians, says Massey. "Supernaturalism is a distinct element in the New Testament accounts. Attempts to tidy up the New Testament by removing such particularities are by necessity ill-fated: the particularities are related to *him*."[11] The claim may seem a bit odd, since Massey takes great pains to argue how credible such a notion would have been to the early believers, and in fact, to the ancient Greco-Roman world, as if their untroubled belief were a mandate for ours. Massey seems to ask us to suspend disbelief *more* rigorously than the apostolic community was required to do.

The fourth consideration in preaching the good news is that Christ is *"the exalted and determinative Person in all creation and history."*[12] This claim is related to Jesus' status as the son of God, but makes universal

---

[8]Ibid., 21.
[9]Ibid., 22.
[10]Ibid., 23.
[11]Ibid., 27.
[12]Ibid., 23. The italics are Massey's.

claims about his authority over all creation and history. Some may find it problematic, in an age of religious pluralism, to make such radical claims for such historic and total uniqueness. One advantage, even though Massey does not avail himself of it, is that claiming universal lordship can at the very least function to encourage Christians to engage in justice-oriented projects all over the world. Massey intends the claim another way, as a mandate for evangelism, since "there is salvation in no one else."[13]

Finally, Massey understands that the original *kerygma* proclaimed Christ as both present and coming. Again, all the warrants are scriptural, but Massey is helpful to indicate why they are still meaningful. Preaching Christ-as-present testifies to the ongoing activity of Christ in the life of the believer and the believing community, and as such, avoids simply reducing the Christ-event to the past tense. Claiming the presence of Christ has significance with regard to worship, granting worship "a depth of affection, moral persuasion, spiritual relation, and contagion" and making the sacraments more than just a backward look.[14] Claiming that the presence of Christ can also endow daily life experience with a sense of purpose and meaning, Massey makes extensive commentary on Paul's use of the phrase "in Christ" as a theological claim about Christ's presence during good times and bad. To be "in Christ," claims Massey, is to understand that a believer's entire life is defined by alliance and agreement with Christ and that the believer is never ultimately alone. If Christ is truly present, we can take comfort during difficult times and give glory during moments of joy.

Christ *is* present with us. Present indeed, either approving or alertly judging by his life. This confrontation is important for us. It helps us to keep the picture of Christ without distortion and our experience with him from diminishing.[15]

Christ is also to be expected in the future, is also always "coming." Massey doesn't use the familiar language of "already and not yet" to discuss modes of presence, but his understanding seems consistent with the claims that while Christ is certainly present, there is a fuller presence expected in the future. The expectation of a future fuller

---

[13]Ibid., 24.

[14]Ibid., 25. It's curious that Massey doesn't make the same claims for resurrection meaning that he makes for kerygmatic presence, but it would be reasonable to assume that the resurrection claims function to proclaim immediate and ongoing presence, in much the same way that kerygmatic presence operates through preaching and sacraments.

[15]Ibid., 26.

presence gives Christians hope, says Massey. The *parousia* is a promise, and as such, provides hope.[16]

Purpose of Preaching

As we have already surveyed in the previous section, the overriding purpose of preaching is to proclaim the good news of salvation through the unique person of Jesus Christ. But Massey also recognizes that beyond the general and fundamental purpose, there are practical purposes as well. "The aim and purpose of the sermon is to educate, edify, and enrich people in the faith."[17] Sermons are supposed to be faith-building, or faith-forming, particularly as moments where Christian truth meets the spiritual needs of sinners by bringing them into the presence of grace. Another purpose for preaching is confrontational; Massey claims that preaching the apostolic kerygma confronts the individual with his or her own salvation in a way that moves them to a decision.

Massey's variety of comments about the purpose of preaching can be characterized as primarily directed toward individuals for their spiritual benefit, however that benefit might be construed. His assumptions embrace an evangelical model as well as a moral edification model, as long as both are understood principally as personal or individual categories. Preaching is to shape individual persons into greater conformity with the life of faith, to bring them into contact with the scriptural "Voice" that speaks of grace, to confront, convict, and save the sinner, and to transform that sinner toward a life of increasing faithfulness. We will see shortly how scripture functions in this regard, but will note for now that preaching speaks to "social" selves, much the same way Jesus' own preaching did, according to claims by Massey.

> The sense of partnership with God helps us to believe that the speech situation can and will *reach* the listener, that it will touch the hearer's life as he knows it...The listener comes as an individual self, but he is also a social self. Preaching must touch him at both levels. Better yet, we must bring the whole man into what we speak, and we must so say it that the hearer will see himself as a whole in the listening act, and react with his whole self to the word of address.[18]

---

[16]Ibid.
[17]Ibid., 67.
[18]Ibid., 82.

So understood, preaching becomes a means of grace for the sinner or for the saved individual in need of deeper understanding or improvement.

Massey also claims that the purpose of preaching is to continue and to participate in the proclamation of Jesus, who preached a personal message of both comfort and confrontation. Whether Jesus' message was pastoral or prophetic, Massey understands it to have been deeply personal and direct, speaking as a Thou to a Thou.[19] Notice that for all the claims about the social nature of selves or about the social demands of Christian belief, Massey's fundamental model is one-to-one, with God (or Jesus Christ) speaking directly to an individual through the activity of biblical preaching.

> Real preaching is rooted in God's concern for persons...real preaching is not merely concerned with the nature of religious experience; it helps the hearer to experience grace, that divine help which deals with human sin and crippling experiences.[20]

This approach is quite consistent with traditional Wesleyan understandings of prevenient grace, justifying grace, and sanctifying grace. Grace can convict, save, and sanctify, but is always directed at individuals for their spiritual welfare. In this understanding, acts of justice or kindness are directed toward the world by believing individuals. We will consider additional implications of Massey's understanding of the purpose of preaching when we turn to his ecclesial assumptions.

Relation between Preaching and Scripture

Preaching from the Bible is necessary, but not adequate alone, claims Massey.[21] Sermons should be biblical. If not text-driven, at the very least they should be informed by biblical theology and particularly by New Testament doctrine. Massey's work in *Designing the Sermon* and in *The Responsible Pulpit* give the most sustained attention to methods of sermon construction informed by the biblical witness. Whether one preaches "on" a text, on a longer passage (expository), or on a topic or

---

[19]Ibid., 98–99. Massey uses the "I-Thou" relational model of Martin Buber when he speaks of what happens during preaching. Massey uses it interchangeably to explore the personal dimension of the believer's encounter with Jesus or with God. See Martin Buber, *I and Thou* (Edinburgh: T. & T. Clark, 1937).

[20]James Earl Massey, *Designing the Sermon: Order and Movement in Preaching* (Nashville: Abingdon Press, 1980), 16.

[21]Ibid., 17.

doctrine, the authoritative "voice" for interpreting meaning is the scriptural word. By using the metaphor of "Voice" to refer to scripture, Massey is claiming that the witness is still living and speaking, and is not solely located to the historical past, as if revelation were over and done with. However, even as he claims that the "Voice" is active, it seems to "speak" exclusively from the pages of scripture.

In his discussion of hermeneutical principles, he begins with the foundational assumption that "meaning is possible through his [*sic*] study of the Bible. The biblical texts were written with purpose; they are materials of signification."[22] He uses Martin Buber's understanding of the "I-Thou" relationship to claim that the Voice originating in the Bible is not an object of study, but a subject with personality and agency whose words interrogate the reader/listener.[23]

His second hermeneutical principle is that the interpreter/listener (the preacher) must be self-critical about his or her own presuppositions, and isolate and suspend them so as to avoid an "unfair" or "popular" cultural interpretation. Massey is adamant that original meaning must be preserved, even as he makes claims elsewhere that preaching is a word-event. We will pursue this discussion later, when we turn to questions of language. For now, it is enough to note that contemporary hermeneutical approaches (Gadamer, Ricoeur, Fuchs, and Ebeling) are quite contrary to Massey's proposal that the preacher/interpreter must divest him- or herself of cultural questions when addressing the original meaning of scripture. This is certainly consistent with his claims about the incredibility of the resurrection and the "problem" of supernaturalism. His third hermeneutical principle lends support: the Bible, as a "holy" book, is its own ultimate authority.[24]

His fourth and fifth hermeneutical principles recognize that the Bible is really two distinct collections of writings involving two different principles of selection. Nevertheless, he considers these two collections and their processes to be unified in message and concern. The unifying principle is that scripture is a product of special revelation.[25]

Massey's sixth hermeneutical principle is critical, and will be treated more extensively in the next section. It follows from his previous five

---

[22]Massey, *The Responsible Pulpit*, 54.
[23]Ibid., 54–55.
[24]Ibid., 55–56.
[25]Ibid., 56–57.

principles and seems to be a logical conclusion to his rhetorical argument (that is what the principles are). His sixth claim assumes that the Bible is authoritative as a special revelation and that *it reveals Jesus as a reinterpreter of the Hebrew Scriptures and rabbinic law.* The argument goes like this: since the biblical witness is authoritative, is unified in its revelatory power, and gives Voice to an authoritative agent, the New Testament witness of Jesus as an authoritative "hermeneut" grants the preacher authority to stand in contrast to the "old" tradition of the rabbis. Massey claims that Jesus' own preaching and interpretive strategies, which subordinated the Old Testament scriptures to allegory or type, is an authoritative model for contemporary preaching. Massey promoted this approach to homiletical hermeneutics more than two decades ago, but has not significantly revised his view on the matter. It is, for Massey, a matter of the authoritative record of scripture that gives us the rationale for different models of interpretation. One of the different (and therefore legitimate) models is the New Testament practice of reading the Old Testament through the eyes of the Christian witness.[26]

His seventh hermeneutical principle deals with language theory. Massey seems to agree with the New Hermeneutic approach, which claims that oral language functions to do more than merely convey facts and information. Language operates on the imagination in a performative way, to actually form a new way of thinking and being in the world. It is not enough, says Massey, to simply study the biblical ideas or biblical contexts as the only clues to interpretation. The preacher must also consider how the language of the text itself performs its task, attending as much to "how" the text says as to "what" it says.[27] These insights, along with rigorous study of biblical languages, will help the preacher recover the original language games and strategies of the biblical writers.[28]

---

[26]Ibid., 57–59.

[27]Ibid., 59–60.

[28]Ibid., 60–62. Readers are encouraged to become familiar with the New Hermeneutic approach to language and interpretation. Massey's interpretation of Fuchs and Ebeling is conservative at best, since it's not accurate that Fuchs and Ebeling or the other New Hermeneutic writers were interested in recovering anything like original meaning. The New Hermeneutic approach made claims contrary to Massey's own, arguing that meaning was generated or produced in the event of hearing, seriously challenging Massey's claim that the "real" meaning is behind the text in its original language. The New Hermeneutic rose in the mid-1960s as a challenge to the Biblical Theology movement and the historical-critical approach Massey seems to prefer. See Gerhard Ebeling, *Word and Faith* (Philadelphia: Fortress Press, 1963) and his *God and Word* (Philadelphia: Fortress Press, 1967). See also Paul Achtemeier, *An Introduction to the New Hermeneutic* (Philadelphia: Westminster Press, 1969).

Relationship between the Testaments

James Massey's hermeneutical principles and his claims about the uniqueness of Jesus Christ locate him in a hermeneutical posture that subordinates the Hebrew Bible to the New Testament. We've already noted that his understanding of Jesus' hermeneutic approach sets Jesus in opposition to certain aspects of his own contemporary religious community and as the self-conscious voice of a new religious truth. Massey seems to be aware of the difficulties of this approach and wants to hold two claims in tension: (1) the uniqueness of Jesus and his message and (2) the continuity of the two testaments and between Jesus and the Law.

He is adamant that the fundamental nature of the good news derives from the status of Jesus as the son of God, and not simply because he was in continuity with the Law and the Prophets.[29]

Massey, for all his historical-critical work, does not question whether Jesus spoke the words attributed to him by the early church, even when questions of attribution might certainly call for a hermeneutic of suspicion. In fact, Massey seems to accept that Jesus saw himself as a special person, with a different ontological status, and as one who fulfilled Israel's messianic expectations.[30] While a fulfillment model is less problematic than a fully discontinuous interpretive approach, it is still a model of superiority.

> [H]is treatment shows that he saw the divine Law in perspective, and he was intent to examine and expose each command in its context for faith, life, and worship. His accent is unmistakable. "But I am saying to you." He preached as God's spokesman. He gave his word with authority and thus showed the supreme

---

[29]Massey, *The Responsible Pulpit*, 95–96.

[30]To be fair, little of Massey's work has been written in the last decade, which has seen a boom in historical Jesus studies. The work of the Jesus Seminar is devoted to a critical and "suspicious" study of the New Testament writings, on the assumption that political and ideological commitments were borne in theological claims about the church, about Jesus Christ, and about doctrinal mandates. The Jesus Seminar scholars are more or less united in their assumptions that few of the sayings attributed to Jesus are authentic. They believe it is more likely that the Jesus sayings are part of the early church's oral tradition, selectively remembered and transmitted to authorize theological and practical commitments. Of particular interest to several Jesus Seminar scholars is the early conflict between the church and the synagogue as a posture demanding claims of Christian uniqueness and superiority.

mark of the man who would bring the Messianic Age, the one who would renew God's covenant with his people.[31]

Most of the themes that characterize a "weak exceptionalism" are present in Massey's work: the uniqueness of Jesus, his divinity, the prophecy/fulfillment paradigm, Jesus as a critic of Judaism, and allegorical and typological approaches.

Nature and Purpose of Faith Communities

Massey's understanding of the relationship between preaching and the church's ministry is a combination of the sanctuary model (which is primary), the evangelistic model (which is secondary), and the civic model (as a third emphasis). Such an understanding is surely consistent with his other homiletical commitments. In LaRue's discussion of the domains for black homiletic theories, Massey would seem to have personal piety, care of the soul, and institutional maintenance as primary preaching concerns.[32]

Personal piety concerns the personal relationship between the believer and God in Christ, the importance of conversion or transformation of self-understanding, and an emotional or psychological relationship between the preacher and the people. LaRue claims that traditional evangelical understandings of personal piety have been appropriated within black preaching with primary emphasis on personal faith and personal formation, marked by a value on "prayer, personal discipline, moral conduct, and the maintenance of a right relationship with God."[33] The *care of the soul* is closely related in its focus on the individual believer in relationship to God, and is directed primarily to issues of comfort and personal healing, to overcoming difficulties and renew a sense of personal wholeness.[34] "The function of sermons preached out of reflection on this domain is to salve or heal the wounds and brokenness of life through some form of encouragement, exhortation, consolation, renewal,

---

[31]Massey, *The Responsible Pulpit*, 96. New Testament scholars will be interested to note that Massey's interpretations of the Jesus sayings are informed by the early work of Norman Perrin, *The Kingdom of God in the Teaching of Jesus* (London: SCM Press, 1963). Perrin's early work used the criterion of "dissimilarity" from intertestamental Judaism as a test for the authenticity of the Jesus sayings and teachings. Such an approach is inherently and self-consciously discontinuous.

[32]Cleophus LaRue, *The Heart of Black Preaching* (Louisville: Westminster John Knox Press, 2000), 20–25.

[33]Ibid., 22.

[34]Ibid.

instruction, or admonishment."[35] The domain involving the *institutional maintenance* of the church is related more to a sense of communal ethos than to specific acts, a sense of belonging to a particular group with identifiable traits and commitments. "Sermons in this domain reflect on the work of the people as a gathered fellowship…how members are to behave and interact with one another and the requirements for spiritual growth and maturity…that gives continued life and sustenance to the institutional church, which in turn reaffirms and upholds its participants."[36]

Massey's homiletical reflections indicate that he sees in-house preaching as first and foremost a function of the sanctuary model, which includes LaRue's domains of personal piety and care of the soul. The sanctuary model assumes that preaching will exist primarily to provide the congregation's membership with opportunities to withdraw from the problems of daily life and take temporary respite in a community of like-minded individuals.[37] Within contemporary homiletic theory (whether African American or white) this orientation draws heavily on a pastoral therapeutic interpretation, offering consolation and emotional safety to its members.

Massey suggests that preaching forms the community one believer at a time by forming mature Christian individuals. "Blessed is the preacher who so speaks as to assure all hearers that God knows and loves each one, that even though facing a crowd, God always has the individual in mind."[38] In the same discussion, Massey cites an author's reflection on John Bunyan's classic in evangelical piety, *Pilgrim's Progress.* Massey valorizes the preacher who can preach to touch people's souls as Massey cites a woman's comment to the preacher, "Sir, your preaching does my soul good."[39]

He claims that the sermon is working most fully for its intended purpose when it counsels or addresses the real-life needs of the hearers. He draws intentional connections between the pastoral theology movement and therapeutic models to urge preachers to speak to the inner experiences of individuals to help clarify their own personal lives and personal commitments. He draws on the insights of Kierkegaardian existentialism to discuss the value of speaking to the subjectivity of the

---

[35]Ibid.
[36]Ibid., 24–25.
[37]See discussion in the introductory chapter.
[38]Massey, *The Burdensome Joy of Preaching,* 34.
[39]Ibid.

hearer. "It is to a listener's inward domain that we preach, and the boundaries of that domain influence his perception, understanding, feelings, choices, and actions. We prepare and preach to enter into that inward domain and arouse the hearer to a whole response to God."[40] The sermon is a means for promoting an inward experience, not necessarily emotional, but nonetheless subjective. Massey even provides a diagram of how the sermonic word is sent and received from one subjectivity (God in Christ) to another (the hearer).[41] Even though Massey clearly understands that the congregation is a group, his model presumes the interaction is one-on-one, almost identical to the communication model.

The preacher's personal integrity and ethos are critical in this interaction, since the message passes through the preacher. Massey's strongest claims about the communal nature of preaching and the church come in his discussion of the minister as a parental figure to the congregation, a father-figure. To the extent that there is a communal identity, it is created by the person of the preacher and his own one-on-one relationships to the individuals in the congregation. The sense of community prevails between preacher and people to the extent that the individuals identify in some way with the preacher.

> This is not only because the preacher holds a learned relationship with the Bible...but also because he holds a living relationship with the assembled group. Standing in a formal but loving relationship with his hearers, the pastor's very presence is itself revealing, and on a most intimate level...The sight of the pastor is always suggesting of sharing, intimacy, membership, family status, guidance, and personal appeal.[42]

The preacher becomes a father-figure to the church community, which is like a family. Massey contends that within the African American tradition, the "analogical significance of the image of father for pastoral work and preaching is crucial" because pastors must exercise parental responsibilities of nurturing, protecting, guiding, and encouraging; the image of fatherly leadership is spiritually essential and psychologically strategic.[43] In relation to LaRue's comments about maintenance of the institutional church, it's easy to see how Massey's model promotes the

---

[40]James Earl Massey, *The Sermon in Perspective: A Study of Communication and Charisma* (Grand Rapids: Baker Book House, 1976), 21.
[41]Ibid., 34.
[42]Ibid., 61.
[43]Ibid., 63.

internal integrity and overall health of the corporate family body, geared for mutuality and service among the family members, for the full functioning of its "family" identity. What is not so clear is whether or not his use of family metaphors commit some of the problems noted by womanist scholars.

In his more recent work *The Burdensome Joy of Preaching*, Massey mentions the work of Henry Mitchell and David Buttrick, claiming that imaginative language may be the key to promoting a sense of mutual mission and identity. We will deal with Massey's comments on language here, rather than separate it from his understanding of community formation. Massey doesn't disagree with claims that ordinary human language unites the preacher and the hearers in a common experience of Christ's presence, but he still maintains that the personal ethos of the preacher is more persuasive to him.[44]

Finally, in discussing his understanding of the relationship of this church family to the world, Massey's understanding seems most consistent with the civic model of the church. Civic models of mission operate on the model of individual citizenship, equipping individuals to see themselves as agents of God's redemptive love.

Preaching and Liturgy

Massey gives little sustained attention to preaching as part of a liturgical event, nor does he attend to issues of sacramental theologies of baptism or the Lord's supper. His claims for the immediate presence of Christ (whether specifically in language, through the person of the preacher, or the act of preaching itself) would certainly provide theological concepts for associating preaching with the sacraments or ordinances of baptism and the communion meal. One might assume, though Massey does not treat it, that the traditional soteriology he claims as the foundation of the gospel might also be manifest in the traditional sacrificial understanding of the meal. His claims about the supernatural elements of New Testament faith might permit him to claim that Christ is present in the meal in the same way he was present at resurrection and in the act of proclamation. This would be consistent with the Wesleyan piety and theology in the Church of God (Anderson) legacy. He could likewise make similar connections to the manifestation

---

[44]Massey, *The Burdensome Joy of Preaching*, 59. Massey cites Henry Mitchell, *The Recovery of Preaching* (San Francisco: Harper & Row, 1977) and David Buttrick, *Homiletic: Moves and Structures* (Philadelphia: Fortress Press, 1987).

of the Holy Spirit in the act of baptism, since the Church of God (Anderson) is part of the broad Holiness movement, assigning significant theological value to the immediate presence of the Holy Spirit.

Nor is there much in Massey's work that hints of ritual studies or understandings of group symbolic behavior.[45] This is probably to be expected and would be consistent with his communication model of language, which tends to reduce the sociological and symbolic dimension of human interaction.

Racial Orientation and African American Studies

We have already noted Massey's claims about the unifying purpose and message of the gospel, so we should not be surprised that Massey downplays differences in preaching traditions. The last chapter of *The Responsible Pulpit*, called "Delivery: Insights From the Black Tradition," is offered to "any preacher from any tradition to sense more clearly how to keep the verbal witness of the pulpit both virile, engaging, and effective."[46]

In this discussion Massey identifies five dimensions of black preaching. He claims that the black sermon is *functional,* in that it is a means to an end and not the end in itself. The black sermon helps to "initiate someone in the faith, instruct some person on how to live, inspire some person to go on living with hope, despite troubles and strain, give insight into problems and possibilities within and beyond those problems...to liberate the hearer's spirit."[47] The black sermon is also *festive* (fun and playful) as well as *climactic* (producing emotion), and both these dimensions coincide with Henry Mitchell's later claims about celebration. Massey draws slightly on James Cone's discussion of African American music to claim that black preaching is *communal* in its musicality and rhythm, as well as in call and response.[48] His brief

---

[45]Massey mentions the value of ritual with regard to funeral sermons, claiming that certain rituals provide comfort and group cohesion. In *Designing the Sermon,* 75–76.

[46]Massey, *The Responsible Pulpit,* 101. The word *virile* is certainly an interesting choice of masculine language for the act of preaching. This is the kind of assumption that African American women preachers and womanist homileticians will reject as they develop their own approaches to homiletics. Similarly, the word *climactic* may also mask some masculine assumptions about homiletic "performance." Women tend to use the metaphors of pregnancy and birth to refer to sermon preparation and delivery. See chapter 7, "African American Women and Womanists."

[47]Ibid., 102.

[48]Ibid., 104. Massey is commenting directly on James Cone, *The Spirituals and The Blues* (New York: Seabury Press, 1972), 5.

discussion of call and response anticipates Evans Crawford's *The Hum,* but Massey is not really making an argument about ritual behavior in quite the same way that Crawford does. Finally, the fifth dimension of black preaching is its *radicality,* or ability to "take the hearer to the roots of personal life and vital response."[49] Massey's claim for radicality does not refer to social radicality, and in fact, disclaims practicing "tribal religion" that "exclude[s] those of another race or color."[50]

The use of the word *tribal* as a pejorative to characterize certain understandings of African American preaching cannot have endeared him to the next generation of African American homileticians. In fact, within two years of Massey's publication of *The Responsible Pulpit* in 1974, Henry Mitchell would review it, lamenting Massey's slight of the African American tradition.[51] Mitchell's own *Black Preaching* had been published four years earlier in 1970, but Massey's only acknowledgment of that book was in a footnote to Massey's own comment that "it has become increasingly current also to speak of a 'black preaching tradition.'"[52]

In August 1994, Henry Mitchell interviewed James Massey for a collection of essays to be published in Massey's honor, and the two discussed their different approaches to African American studies and homiletics. Massey told Mitchell:

> I have felt no compelling need to plow ground you have so ably covered. Instead, my concern has been to share with the wider church the homiletical emphases we both love and teach...working as I have done "within the white tradition," as you put it, I consciously chose an approach by which our black preaching particularity could be taught, modeled, assessed, and hopefully, adopted. To this end it was wiser to treat our pulpit peculiarities within the wider context of preaching approaches. With me it has never been a matter of living at the extreme of no recognition of my black heritage or the opposite extreme of emphasizing only the black heritage...I remain convinced that my bicultural approach has helped me to be reasonable, realistic, relational, and effective.[53]

---

[49]Ibid., 105.

[50]Ibid.

[51]Henry Mitchell, in *Homiletic: A Review of Publications in Religious Communication,* I (1976), listings 9 and 10.

[52]Massey, *The Responsible Pulpit,* 101.

[53]Callen, *Sharing Heaven's Music,* 216–17.

Massey's theological commitment to general human unity, to Christian ecumenism, and what he calls "the relational teachings of Jesus" lead him to this posture.

Homiletic Method

Massey's sermons demonstrate variety of form, but rarely of content or strategy. Each sermon is devoted primarily to explicating the text; even his narrative sermons adhere closely to the textual world and characters with little in the way of contemporary contextualizing. His sermons have an almost timeless quality to them, since there is so little commentary on contemporary life or issues.

He uses relatively few illustrations, and when he does, they are more frequently a sentence or two drawn from "great lives" (usually from the Western tradition: Cicero, Martin Luther, Origen, John Dewey, Thomas à Kempis) than something from ordinary life. He is similar to Gardner Taylor in this regard, suggesting an inspirational purpose behind the illustrations. Taylor tends to balance his sermons with illustrations from ordinary contemporary life and the sciences as well, drawing the worlds together more than Massey does.

In a sermon published after the 1994 Mitchell interview, Massey used an extended illustration about some boys who painted a Catholic statue of Jesus black. The statue was in front of the Sacred Heart Seminary just down the street from where Albert Cleage had been preaching about the Black Messiah. What's interesting about Massey's use of the illustration is that he refers to the boys as "vandals" and to the white Catholic officials as "wise" for letting the black paint remain. In an illustration employing the words "Black Messiah" and "Albert Cleage," it's notable that Massey did not actually engage in any racial polemic, but managed to salvage the story without creating any villains. He concludes the illustration by assessing the black Jesus as a positive, "as a witness that Jesus is related to all, that he is the inclusive Christ who must always be understood beyond color and race considerations."[54] Since Massey could have told this story any number of ways, the way he chose to characterize the two groups demonstrates his own conciliatory agenda. Language is loaded.

---

[54]Massey, *The Burdensome Joy of Preaching,* 94–95.

Massey occasionally quotes poetry, but more frequently quotes hymn lyrics. His use of language is somewhat scholarly and precise, and occasionally quite abstract. He rarely uses repetition, alliteration, or extended metaphors.

5

James Alexander Forbes, Jr.

James Alexander Forbes, Jr., a self-described "progressive Pentecostal," is currently the senior pastor of Riverside Church in New York City. Riverside Church, long identified with famous preachers, is affiliated with the American Baptist Churches in the U.S.A. and the United Church of Christ, and has been led by such prominent preachers as William Sloane Coffin and Harry Emerson Fosdick. Forbes, the first African American senior pastor of Riverside, came to that pulpit after pastoring in Virginia, North Carolina, and New York, and after teaching homiletics at Union Theological Seminary, also in New York.

He was born in Burgaw, North Carolina in 1935, to Mable and James A. Forbes, who was also a Pentecostal preacher. The younger Forbes was called into ministry while a medical student and holds earned degrees from Howard University (B.S. in Chemistry, 1957), Union Theological Seminary (B.D., 1962), and Colgate-Rochester Divinity School (D.Min., 1975). He was ordained into the Original United Holy Church International and served a number of parishes. In 1976, Forbes was named Brown-Sockman Associate Professor of Preaching at Union. In 1984 he was named by *Ebony* magazine as one of the top fifteen African American preachers in America, and in 1986 was promoted to Joe R.

Engle Professor of Preaching at Union. He assumed the pulpit at Riverside in 1989.[1]

In addition to many published sermons, Forbes has written a number of articles on the nature of the church and its social ministry and on the doctrine of the Holy Spirit; in 1986 he delivered the esteemed Lyman Beecher Lectures at Yale. His Beecher Lectures were published in 1989 under the title *The Holy Spirit and Preaching.* Forbes is a much sought-after college and conference speaker, and is also frequently quoted in the New York and national press for his progressive blend of Christian faith and social activism. His call to Riverside Church was originally perceived as a conciliatory move combining traditional spirituality and social justice.[2] His own tenure at Riverside has been no less marked by controversy than that of his predecessor, William Sloane Coffin.

Nature of the Gospel

Forbes identifies his theology as "progressive pentecostalism [with] a strong emphasis on spirit but deep commitment to transformative social action."[3] The key to Forbes's theological project is the relationship between the Holy Spirit and the vocation of Jesus. Forbes argues that the Spirit was what gave content and energy to Jesus' messianic and prophetic vocation, enabling him to proclaim a new social order ordained by God. The Spirit anoints Jesus, authorizing and nurturing him for the ministry of proclaiming the kingdom of God.

Forbes's distinction between the vocation of Jesus and his identity is a helpful one for preachers. While Forbes does in fact argue for a thoroughgoing divinity and uniqueness for Jesus, this ontological issue is not the one he emphasizes. The work of the Spirit, whether in the life and ministry of Jesus or in the life and ministry of the church, is to unmask the powers and principalities operative in ordinary sociopolitical life, to disclose the contours of real social and political liberation, to project God's hopes for a reconciled world, to witness to those glimmers of hope, and to equip ordinary humans for ministries of discernment, critique, and renunciation. In this sense, personal spirituality is not some amorphous religious feeling, but an inner attitude with definite marks,

---

[1]Biographical information from Larry G. Murphy, J. Gordon Melton, Gary L. Ward, eds., *Encyclopedia of African American Religions* (New York: Garland, 1993), 274–75.

[2]Murphy et al., eds., *Encyclopedia of African American Religions,* 275.

[3]James A. Forbes, Jr., *The Holy Spirit and Preaching* (Nashville: Abingdon Press, 1989), 15.

the primary one of which is to rise above preoccupation with self-interest and self-protection. This understanding of personal spirituality extends to what might be called a corporate or congregational spirituality, where the guiding principle for group behavior is to transcend the group's self-interest or survival. Without this sense of the sacred, says Forbes, we might expect the church to conform to secular patterns of self-understanding, self-promotion, and tribalism. "Given the reality of a culture that has lost contact with the living Spirit of the one who announced to us the vision of the kingdom in the first place, we need preaching that is more than aesthetically delightful. Mere ranting and raving and excitation from some spirited pastor will not suffice."[4]

What is most critical to remember about Forbes's pneumatological approach is the necessary relationship between the Spirit's promptings and the proclamation of the kingdom. Forbes presents an interpretation of the inauguration of Jesus' ministry to establish the connection between the Spirit and the kingdom in Jesus' own preaching. When Jesus claimed the anointing of the Spirit, he claimed it in the context of a religious community and for the purpose of preaching a particular message to a particular sociopolitical reality. The Spirit does not just anoint uncritically or generally, but anoints for the purpose of announcing a certain kind of ministry to a certain kind of community. In Luke 4:18 Jesus claims to be anointed by the Spirit, to preach good news to the poor and liberation for captives. Anointing is specific. Besides making a claim about himself, Jesus made specific claims about the nature of his own ministry and the kingdom he came to announce.[5] Being anointed, claims Forbes, is being authorized to act as a representative of God. The prophets of the Hebrew Bible understood their prophetic proclamations to be part of their anointing for a prophetic ministry. This understanding of anointing for a particular vocation is continuous between the testaments, is what Jesus was claiming for his own ministry, and is how the first apostles understood their ministries.[6]

---

[4]Ibid., 25.

[5]I might take exception to Forbes's assumption that Jesus is claiming some unique kind of anointing or any special status. See my argument about the New Testament understandings of divinity in *Trouble with Jesus: Women, Christology, and Preaching* (St. Louis: Chalice Press, 1999), 42–54.

[6]Forbes refers to Peter's sermon in Acts 10, and especially to verses 36–38, "You know the word which is sent to Israel, preaching good news of peace by Jesus Christ...how God anointed Jesus...and how he went about doing good and healing all that were oppressed by the devil."

By offering this clear understanding of the Spirit and its work, Forbes connects the nature of the proclamation with the person of Jesus, the purposes of God, the mode of the Spirit, and the vocation of the church. The good news is continuous with Jesus' proclamation of the Jewish prophetic impulse: God's project is no less than a radical transformation of sociopolitical life and the liberation of the economically and politically disenfranchised.

Purpose of Preaching

Because of his starting point in pneumatology, Forbes is well-situated for a robust theory of preaching. In some ways, Forbes sees preaching as an extension of that "ordinary" discipleship to which all Christians are called: the ministry of witness in word and deed, discernment according to theological commitments, spiritual energy, and alertness to signs of promise. More than anything, Forbes provides interpretive guidelines for discerning the activity of the Spirit and its leading.

Preaching involves the articulation of this activity of discernment; preaching is primarily a highly contextualized act of interpretation. Preaching focuses the "dialogue between God and the people in the context of worship" and is consistent and continuous with the preaching of Jesus.[7] Preaching proclaims the gospel or the good news of God's kingdom hopes for social transformation. Proclamation invites people to enter the family of faith and has evangelical or conversion purposes, but Forbes's theology of proclamation attends more to the nurturing and empowering dimension of preaching that is directed to the already baptized. Preaching "calls to maturity and faithfulness those who have committed their lives to the lordship of Jesus the Christ…[and empowers them] to serve and to celebrate the present and coming kingdom of God."[8] Preaching is an act that addresses the congregation, motivates it to turn toward the world, and engenders an attitude of patience, respect, and advocacy for those who are disenfranchised. The purpose of preaching is to be radical and countercultural and to involve the congregation in ministry to the world.[9] In this regard, "the world is our parish," claims Forbes.[10] The gospel is for liberation and transformation that aims beyond the immediate needs of the local congregation.

---

[7] Forbes, *The Holy Spirit and Preaching*, 56.

[8] Ibid.

[9] James A. Forbes, Jr., "Preaching in the Contemporary World," in *For Creation's Sake: Preaching, Ecology, and Justice*, ed. Dieter T. Hessel (Philadelphia: Geneva Press, 1985), 48–49.

[10] Forbes, "Preaching in the Contemporary World," 52.

However, preaching is more than just a "discourse on religious subjects." Preaching is an event where the living word of God becomes present to the hearers; preaching is one significant way that God continues to communicate with believers. Rather than elevating the preacher to some special status, this understanding demands that the preacher stand under the authority and humility of the word.[11] A true understanding of spiritual presence and anointing teaches believers, and particularly preachers, that pride, ego, and self-confidence are misplaced in Christian discipleship. Even though Forbes doesn't directly address the fruits of the spirit in his major works on homiletical theory, he seems to suggest the Pauline virtues of humility, patience, and self-control. He calls this a "pneumatological epistemology" or a Spirit-directed way of knowing that is always self-critical and suspicious of personal benefits.[12] The preacher must be an anointed believer, trusting in the Spirit and humbled in his or her own pretensions. The anointing of the preacher is critical for preaching to be an inspired word of God.

If the purpose of the divine word (to create a just world) is the ideal toward which preaching and all Christian ministry is directed, the reality is that we live in a world characterized by other values and forces. It is not enough for a preacher to envision God's reconciled world and to look out for signs and hints of true reconciliation. The preacher who is anointed and has the discernment afforded by the Spirit will be attentive to what the people say and experience. The anointed preacher will recognize death in all its power and subtlety. "Preaching is bearing witness to the resurrecting power of God, which extends itself into the regions of death, so that the new life in Christ breaks forth in all dimensions of the created order."[13] This dimension of preaching is what Forbes refers to as "the ministry of raising the dead."[14] This ministry prevents preachers from superficial proclamation, demanding that they remain in the midst of death. Forbes uses the narrative of Ezekiel's prophesying to the dry bones as an image for this ministry of hope to the hopeless. The purpose of the gospel, and therefore of preaching, is to restore life to the church that is coopted by secular values of greed,

---

[11]See also Forbes's discussion of the necessity for lay preachers within each community of believers, in "What Is Preaching?–A Response," in *A New Look At Preaching*, ed. John Burke, O.P. (Wilmington, Del.: Michael Glazier, 1983), 128, 131.

[12]Forbes, *The Holy Spirit and Preaching*, 49.

[13]Ibid., 56.

[14]Ibid., 58.

competition, and self-interest.[15] The message is to be ecumenical as well as universal. God wants all creation to come to abundant life.

Relationship between Preaching and Scripture

Forbes's pneumatological hermeneutic is the key to his appropriation of the Bible in preaching. While Forbes does preach regularly from the lectionary, he also preaches topically and thematically, and does so from his theological norms of the gospel.[16] It's fair to say that Forbes doesn't preach "on" a text as much as he uses a text to preach the message of the gospel. Forbes tends to preach within the broad biblical themes we've already identified as consistent with his understanding of the gospel. His use of the Bible is a prophetic use that calls for real historical liberation, freedom for the oppressed, and good news for the poor. He also frequently appeals to biblical themes of a diverse and beloved creation, the creation of humans in the *imago dei,* and the radical equality of all individuals. His eschatological themes include the promises of a restored land and a restored human and nonhuman community.

Notice that Forbes doesn't necessarily begin with the Bible as the "content provider" for preaching. This term from the world of electronic information is helpful. A content provider is the agent who provides the raw stuff or material for electronic delivery and manipulation. Many homiletic theories treat the scriptural canon as the content provider for preaching: scripture is the stuff we deliver. Forbes actually tends to reverse the pattern of recent modernity, and especially of Karl Barth and the neoorthodox and postliberals. Forbes's insistence that preaching is an act of interpreting God's *current* word severs the assumed necessary relationship between preaching and past revelation. No one familiar with Forbes's written work, public sermons, or published sermons would ever claim that scripture is irrelevant or uninspired. However, Forbes's appreciation of the scripture seems to be driven by his claims about the nature and purposes of the God revealed therein, and not a claim about the nature of the text itself.[17] "Preaching is an event

---

[15]Forbes, "What Is Preaching?–A Response," 129.

[16]James A. Forbes, Jr., interview, *Great Preachers Series,* no. 6, Odyssey Productions Ltd. (Worchester, Pa. : Gateway Films/Vision Video, 1997).

[17]Forbes is quite clear about the influences on his own theological development. He studied at Union Theological Seminary from 1958 to 1962. He studied Hebrew Bible with James Muilenburg, New Testament with John Knox, and theological ethics with Reinhold Niebuhr. Forbes admits that Paul Tillich's third volume of *Systematic Theology,* presented by the theologian himself in James Chapel, intrigued him. Early in his career, Forbes referred to himself as a "Tillichian Pentecostal."

in which the *living* word of God is proclaimed in the power of the Holy Spirit."[18]

This approach allows Forbes to consider other than traditional theological resources and Biblical proof-texting. He tends to operate with a certain hermeneutic of suspicion toward the parts of the Bible that might support exclusionary practices, self-righteousness, or attitudes of condemnation. Forbes is convinced that the authoritative truth of the Bible is God's unconditional love for all creation, God's attempts to renew and restore the integrity of all creation, and the church's mandate to manifest God's love and reconciliation in practices of justice.[19] He frequently takes positions that would be characterized as progressive or socially liberal, calling for eco-justice, gay and lesbian rights, distribution of material resources, and a radical social commitment to the common good.[20]

It's not enough for preachers to know the biblical worldview, claims Forbes. Ministers should know the real worldview of contemporary culture and how the mandate for compassion and reconciliation critiques cultural values. He uses the mythological language of powers and principalities to critique contemporary social dysfunction. Here is where Forbes's own hermeneutic bears homiletic fruit, since the preacher must identify the contemporary powers and principalities that deceive and destroy life. Forbes demythologizes the mysterious apocalyptic categories of the New Testament in terms of Old Testament prophetic insight. The powers and principalities include imperialism, utilitarian expressionism, exploitation and discrimination, apartheid in South Africa, homophobia, militarism, racism, sexism, and materialism.[21] However, even as preachers are called to be prophetic critics of both the church and the culture, there is no margin for self-righteousness.

Preachers will frequently find themselves involved in a hermeneutical circle: in conversation with the Bible, with traditional doctrinal understandings, with the contemporary culture, and with the particular congregation. Forbes assumes that a preacher concerned about the real world will have contact with that real world to understand the way politics, media, education, and the arts function to project values and

---

[18]Forbes, *The Holy Spirit and Preaching*, 56, emphasis mine.
[19]Forbes, "Preaching in the Contemporary World," 45–46.
[20]Forbes, "Matters of the Heart," *Sojourners* 18, no. 5 (May 1989): 26; "Whatever Happened to the Golden Rule?," in *Envisioning the New City: A Reader on Urban Ministry,* ed. Eleanor Scott Meyers (Louisville: Westminster/John Knox Press, 1992), 93.
[21]Forbes, "Matters of the Heart," 25–26.

advocate for particular behaviors. Writing about the eco-justice movement, he claims that preachers frequently don't make the connections between poverty and ecology because they don't take cultural analysis or critical thinking seriously. Materialism, escalating impoverishment, and the rape of the environment are all fundamentally related. Preachers have to know their contexts. We preach to postmodern people in a postmodern and complex world. Preachers need to address the real world of their hearers if they hope to be the current breath of the Spirit.

Relationship between the Testaments

Even though Forbes doesn't directly tackle a discussion about the relationship between the testaments, it's fair to assume from his own theological positions that the message and prophetic character of Jesus are consistent with the message of the First Testament. He doesn't set up oppositions between Judaism and Christianity; nor does he use the language of prophecy/fulfillment or law/gospel. It's not clear how critical Jesus' own status is to Forbes's articulation of anointing. He seems to claim that while Jesus' anointing was unique, its uniqueness is not its authority. In fact, if Forbes is consistent all the way through, the work of the Spirit would have to be continuously witnessing to the same theological truth in both testaments in order to be authoritative. It is not anything about Jesus' special status that authorizes the ministry of the church. If Jesus' own anointing is to be a model for us, it cannot be in a superhuman category.

Nature and Purpose of Faith Communities

The vocation of the church is to serve the world.[22] The church is made up of those baptized believers who join the work of the Holy Spirit in restoring all of God's creation to its intended integrity. The church's evangelical purpose is to work toward the realization of the kingdom of God, which is much more than the establishment and growth of worldwide Christianity. The church is not the kingdom, but works in the world for kingdom purposes: to stand in solidarity with the poor and oppressed, to advocate for justice, and to speak the truth in love. Forbes uses the language of blessing to speak to the peculiar vocation

---

[22]Forbes, "What Is Preaching?" 132.

of the church. "The community that I came up in had the understanding that if God had blessed you, you at least ought to have the common decency to invest in some things that God is concerned about."[23]

Forbes's ecclesiology is radically ecumenical and tolerant, and his commitment to ecumenicity is consistent with his understanding of the work of the Holy Spirit. The golden rule for congregations is not just a congregational or denominational or even a Christian identity issue.[24] Forbes suggests a theology of radical hospitality that invites and appreciates the faith perspectives of those within Christianity as well as outside of it. The commitments of Christians must transcend narrow boundaries to work for the common good of the entire human and nonhuman community. What distinguishes the church is that we engage in our projects in the name of Jesus the Christ, and not in some other name.

The church is a critical context for discerning the Spirit's direction in particular situations and locations. The church is the place where we bring all our faith claims and our cultural analysis and our political commitments together in order to identify the contemporary demands of discipleship.[25] Church is not a private experience, but a communal one; preachers must speak to the group identity of believers to form them for serving the world. At the same time, the commitments and activities of churches are subject to the same critique and challenge that we might direct toward the ordinary culture. The church is neither perfect nor perfectible; it is likewise overadapted to the world and tempted by the powers and principalities.[26]

Forbes's ecclesiology is clearly in the activist model. The activist orientation assumes that the world is God's arena and that the church is called to be an advocate for the world that God loves. Forbes places a high priority on social justice, social critique, and proactive challenge to existing economic and political structures. His homiletic focus is dominantly this-worldly, prophetic, and collective, geared toward moving the community toward a shared commitment and action.

---

[23]Forbes, "Matters of the Heart," 25.
[24]Forbes, "Whatever Happened to the Golden Rule?" 92–97; "Preaching in the Contemporary World," 52–53.
[25]Forbes, "What Is Preaching?" 128.
[26]Ibid.

Preaching and Liturgy

Forbes insists that preaching and the liturgical context both function to create an experience of the presence of God through the Holy Spirit. Preaching and the sacraments both mediate God's presence and both are means of grace.[27] They are united by a theology of celebration and joy, and both operate to open up believers to the encouragement of the Spirit. "Both Word and sacrament are occasions when heightened attentiveness to divine presence touch[es] deeper dimensions of our lives and call[s] forth freeing expressions of gratitude and devotion."[28]

Again, Forbes's focus is ecumenical, traditional, and radical. He refuses to reduce liturgy and the sacramental life to mere ritual or formalism when he argues that the aesthetics of a compelling sermon and of a eucharistic celebration move the imagination. He values the diversity within the Christian tradition and appreciates the way that some denominations have kept either preaching or liturgy vibrant. This appreciation leads him to urge preachers to keep preaching, liturgy, and sacraments together, calling the church to "serious balance and maintenance of Word and sacrament." He doesn't advocate a slavish devotion or a careless rejection of ancient patterns. We should be open, in the Spirit, to whatever value there is in traditional forms as well as in contemporary forms. "The humility to mature within and beyond limiting perspectives of past formulations is a mark of the spiritual church."[29]

Racial Orientation and African American Studies

Forbes offers a gentle criticism of his own theological education for its failure to teach about the heritage of the black church, noting, however, that not even black seminaries of that era considered such instruction a priority.[30] In his typical ecumenical spirit, Forbes advocates for explicit inclusion of African American faculty members, and particularly those of Pentecostal heritage. He argues that diversity within the student body and within the faculty should transcend tokenism and reflect a genuine variety of black perspectives.

---

[27] Ibid., 133.
[28] Ibid.
[29] Ibid., 132.
[30] James A. Forbes, Jr., "Ministry of Hope from a Double Minority," *Theological Education* 9 suppl (Summer 1973): 313.

He expresses strong appreciation for the historic black church and for the "black prophets of the sixties," who nurtured a positive sense of black identity. He claims that African American churches sustained and nurtured generations of believers and that without this resource, "the present strength [and liberation] of our people would have been impossible."[31]

Forbes frequently uses understandings and language of James Cone, his Union colleague. Like Cone, Forbes writes regularly of God's advocacy for the oppressed and the themes of liberation theology. Still, he cautions against any understanding that God has a *preferential* option for the oppressed or that Jesus was "ontologically black." God has no preferences as regards individuals, but only for justice and reconciliation. "When I say that 'God is the God of the oppressed,' I mean that God is the God of those who are obviously oppressed, and God also is the God of those who are oppressed but who do not yet know it...the gospel also addresses those people who think that God is on their side by virtue of their prosperity and the power they enjoy."[32]

Even as he appreciates the strengths of the black church, Forbes cautions against romanticizing it or black history. He allows that the black church is no less subject to the powers and principalities than any other human community. "Let us dispense with recounting the 'glorious past' of this great black church."[33] Forbes worries that there is not a realistic or humble balance between being "black-shy" and ashamed of racial history and engaging in the "idolatrous gospel of blackness."[34] He also expresses misgivings about ministers who reduce liberation to materialistic self-interest as well as those ministers who preach passivity and spiritual escapism. Forbes claims that among the challenges facing the black church is the development of an "adequate black Christian education" program that will teach liberation and social advocacy. In relation to this mission, black churches will have to find ways to secure finances for something beyond church growth and building projects. Stewardship for liberation projects will carry the church's mission beyond its own four walls and into the world.[35]

---

[31]Ibid., 314.
[32]Forbes, "Matters of the Heart," 25.
[33]Forbes, "A Ministry of Hope," 314.
[34]Ibid., 315.
[35]Ibid., 315–16.

Preaching and Language Studies

Forbes doesn't explicitly employ language theories in his homiletic approach, but does demonstrate some attention to their influence on his understanding of preaching. He claims that preaching is a "speech-event," wherein the present situation and experience of the hearers "enables the text to yield up nuances of meaning not explicitly grasped before."[36] *Speech-event* is the term used by language theorists and homileticians to refer to a phenomenon peculiar to oral/aural presentation. Amos Wilder, following Ernst Fuchs, claims that the gospels in particular are characterized not only by their content but by the performative nature of the language used to disclose religious meaning. The use of certain types of language and the ways of using language can open up dimensions of understanding that were previously masked. Speaking is direct, rhetorically oriented toward a particular situation and audience, immediate, and temporary. The immediacy of oral language performs the same way that direct communication from God was understood to perform. The act of speech not only addresses the hearers but calls for a response.

It might be fair to assume that Forbes understands preaching as a speech-event precisely because of his assumptions about the activity of the Holy Spirit as an immediate presence in the act of proclamation. Preaching is a speech-event, not because it talks about a past-tense experience or understanding, but because it creates an immediate present-tense experience. In this regard, Forbes associates preaching with liturgy and the sacraments, speaking of a kind of "aesthetic" understanding. Forbes never rejects the role of emotion in preaching, but neither does he reduce the purpose of language to the production of emotion. "There are no raw experiences that amount to direct discoveries of God apart from an interpretive element. The interpretation is neither prior to nor subsequent to the experience, but is rather intrinsic and indigenous to it."[37] Along with Taylor, Forbes seems to suggest that the "how" of language is as critical as the "what" of its content, and that language works more on the imagination and understanding than on the emotions. Forbes claims that preaching moves people by its careful use of language, imagination, and persuasion. He advocates the use of strong verbs to effect lifestyle changes and subtle suggestion to transform outlook.[38]

---

[36]Forbes, "What Is Preaching?" 128.
[37]Ibid.
[38]Forbes, "Preaching in the Contemporary World," 49.

Again, Forbes understands that all this care and preparation are overseen by the Spirit, who hovers during exegesis, word studies, the selection of illustrations, and the determination of sermon structure. The Spirit does not wait until the moment of delivery and then spring forward in bursts of emotion, but has the freedom to operate subtly in all dimensions of study, preparation, and analysis.

Homiletic Method

Forbes's own homiletic strategies are extremely eclectic. Like Taylor, he uses a variety of rhetorical styles within any one sermon, but uses vernacular and colloquialism more frequently than any of the other homileticians except for Henry Mitchell. From a published sermon for Christmas, Forbes refers to the genuine human misery experienced in the midst of the holiday season, saying, "During these days of December, even when the twenty-fifth finally arrives, there are still people who are deciding that they're not going to play the game and, therefore, either break up, crack up, or hang it up."[39] Forbes uses humor and irony more frequently than the other preachers in this survey. Within the same sermon, he characterizes our desire for honor: "We want the Good Housekeeping Seal of Moral Rectitude from our families and our communities."[40]

Forbes also demonstrates even more variety in selecting illustrations than does Taylor, drawing on immediate social and political issues. Where Massey's sermons could hardly be pinned down as to their date of delivery, Forbes's sermons are so highly contextualized as to be datable within a period of a few weeks or months. During the late 1980s he regularly preached quite specifically against South African apartheid and American economic complicity in that system. From a sermon delivered from the Riverside Pulpit in 1997, Forbes made specific comments about then-President Bill Clinton, referring to recent welfare legislation.[41]

Forbes regularly uses intentional rhythm and cadence, alliteration, and repetition. He also uses a great deal of personal testimony in his sermons, frequently ending with highly emotional confessions of faith and commitment. In the Christmas sermon, he devotes an extensive

---

[39]James A. Forbes, Jr., "The Battle of Bethlehem," in *Outstanding Black Sermons,* vol. 3, ed. Milton E. Owens, Jr. (Valley Forge, Pa.: Judson Press, 1982), 28.

[40]Forbes, "The Battle of Bethlehem," 32.

[41]Forbes, *Great Preachers.*

part of his conclusion (what would amount to about six or seven minutes) to his own personal confession. Here's a sample from the end of his testimonial:

> Jesus, you're my Lord because I'm willing to take my cues from you. I'm willing to take orders from you. I'm willing to receive encouragement from you. I'm willing to participate with you in this cosmic battle between the kingdoms. Jesus, I have confidence in you; my hope rests in you. You are my hero; you are my leader. And I'm going to stick with you.[42]

Forbes is a significant homiletic figure for his explicit articulation of particular social justice themes and his attempts at contextualizing. When we turn to a discussion of African American women scholars and particularly the womanist scholars, we will see similar commitments to particular social justice issues.

---

[42]Forbes, "The Battle of Bethlehem," 35.

6

Henry Herbert Mitchell

Henry Herbert Mitchell was born in Columbus, Ohio, in 1920, to Orlando W. Mitchell and Bertha Estis Mitchell. Grandson of two Baptist preachers, he recognized his call to ministry by the time he was fourteen, but claims that he doesn't know of a time when he didn't believe in God "or the need to be led by the Word of God."[1] He attended college at Ohio State and at Lincoln University, and studied for the ministry at Union Theological Seminary in New York City. He was shaped by some of the biggest names in theological education in the 1940s: Reinhold Niebuhr, Paul Tillich, Harry Emerson Fosdick, and George Buttrick. Even the quality of that theological education could not allay Mitchell's conviction that something was missing from mainstream white theological education: attention to black experience and black culture.

Before he began his sustained attention to the African American preaching tradition, Mitchell served (from 1945–1959) the General

---

[1]Martha J. Simmons, ed., *Preaching on the Brink: The Future of Homiletics: In Honor of Henry H. Mitchell* (Nashville: Abingdon Press, 1996), 17. This volume is dedicated to Mitchell and contains essays by prominent homileticians, including one by James Earl Massey.

Baptist Association of Northern California, the Northern California Baptist Convention, and the American Baptist Churches Home Missionary Society. His first full-time pastorate was at Second Baptist Church in Fresno, California, where his serious interest in homiletics emerged. He studied linguistics at Fresno State College, and after six years at Second Baptist, he took another church.

However, by 1969, he had already established himself as an author and popular speaker, and accepted a position at Colgate Rochester Divinity School as the Martin Luther King, Jr., Professor of Black Church Studies. In 1970, he published *Black Preaching.* He earned a Doctor of Theology Degree from Claremont School of Theology, and in 1974, delivered the Lyman Beecher Lectures at Yale. His lectures were printed as *The Recovery of Preaching.* In 1975, he published *Black Belief.*

He and his wife, Ella Pearson Mitchell, founded and directed the Ecumenical Center for Black Church Studies in Los Angeles. He has taught at Colgate Rochester Divinity School. From 1982 to 1986, Mitchell was Dean of Virginia Union Seminary, and from 1988 to 1995 he team-taught homiletics with Ella Mitchell at the Interdenominational Theological Center in Atlanta. In 1989 he began teaching in the doctor of ministry program at United Theological Seminary in Dayton, Ohio, and in 1990 he published *Celebration and Experience in Preaching.* His most recent publications are coauthored and include *Preaching for Black Self-Esteem* (1994) with Emil Thomas, and *Together for Good* (1999), an autobiographical work with wife Ella Mitchell. In 2000, Henry and Ella Mitchell were copresidents of the Academy of Homiletics, the primary professional guild for those who teach and research homiletics. He is currently on the editorial board of *The African American Pulpit,* a journal devoted exclusively to sermons and homiletic insights from the African American preaching tradition.

Mitchell is a significant figure in African American homiletics, not only for the volume of his scholarship and his devotion to teaching preaching, but for being the first African American homiletician to formulate explicitly Afrocentric interpretations and norms for preaching. Afrocentricity is described as an interpretive approach grounded in a non-dualistic, communal, materialistic intersubjectivity that characterizes African philosophy. African anthropology is strongly positive; ethics is primarily communal as opposed to Christian European emphasis upon private morality. According to Molefe Kete Asante, "The Afrocentrist seeks to uncover and use codes, paradigms, symbols, motifs, myths, and circles of discussion that reinforce the centrality of African ideals and values as a valid frame of reference for acquiring and examining data."[2] Mitchell's earliest books, *Black Preaching* (1970) and *The Recovery of Preaching* (1977), were written as James Cone was inaugurating a public academic black theology. Mitchell was aware of Cone's work during the writing of *Black Preaching,* and it's clear that Cone's work had influence on Mitchell, even if it is not clear how much interdependence there was in the development of their self-consciously African American approaches. Mitchell's position as a self-consciously African American homiletician marks a watershed in the tradition's approach to homiletic theory. Since his theories are so thoroughly informed by African American context and studies, this category will be dealt with throughout instead of in a separate section.

Nature of the Gospel

True to his Baptist and evangelical commitments, Mitchell's articulations of the gospel are centered on claims of grace, mercy, and the love of God. However, Mitchell distinguishes his theological claims from traditional Baptist piety and from what he calls "white orthodoxy" by claiming that traditional notions of human sinfulness and depravity have been overemphasized. This overemphasis has led to internalized low self-esteem among African Americans, and has contributed more to oppression than to liberation. Without denying the tradition's claims, Mitchell hopes to reclaim a more holistic and contextual faith that addresses the actual problems of African Americans: social marginality and distorted self-understandings.

To this end, he centers his understanding on claims about theological anthropology. Humans may have tendencies for sin, but they are also made in the image of God, and therefore God desires humans to reach their full potential and to enjoy abundant life within history.

> For the oppressed and the depressed, this is the kind of healing word and emphasis that is required. And this sort of nourishment for the crushed spirit can be found throughout the Bible...The entire ministry of Jesus was devoted to the liberation, healing, and affirming of people who had both low social status and low self-esteem.[3]

---

[2]See Molefe Kete Asante, *Kemet, Afrocentricity and Knowledge* (Trenton: African World Press, 1990), 3, and chapter 1, "Interiors."

[3]Henry H. Mitchell and Emil M. Thomas, *Preaching for Black Self-Esteem* (Nashville: Abingdon Press, 1994), 33.

In response to the potential charge that self-esteem and self-love are antithetical to a piety of self-denial, Mitchell and Thomas claim that the two postures are not in opposition, but are actually complementary. Self-denial is not total martyrdom, but rather "a refusal to be controlled by one's lesser pleasures and self-centered interests—a refusal to let lower goals and lesser priorities crowd out the larger concerns of the kingdom of God. It is in these concerns or 'crosses' that one finds complete fulfillment. This is the highest form of self-affirmation."[4]

The love of God, self, and neighbor are "all inextricably bound together," and Mitchell claims that the abundant life promised in the biblical story is grounded on this holistic love. Sin plays a certain role in keeping us from this abundant life, and Mitchell elsewhere concedes that "Yes, Virginia, there is such a thing as sin," but one of the ways sin functions socially is in its ability to create in us a false image (experience) of ourselves and others.[5] The false experience may come from bad theology, bad parenting, or social deprivation, but it holds us hostage to anxiety and low expectations. The gospel is decidedly *good* news, and Mitchell urges preachers to offer more gospel positives than negatives.

> People cannot actually be glad about what does not exist, or what is wrong, or what ought to be, no matter how justified the criticism may be...Only positive truths about God through Christ give healing and empowerment, causing great rejoicing and praise...Preaching's accentuation of the positive Good News should help hearers to be liberated from this dead hand of the cultural past, as well as to seek by faith and work to liberate the oppressed.[6]

The good news is that God loves us and wants the best possible life for all human beings. For Mitchell, this biblical truth is dominant in the First Testament and is what is manifested through the ministry of Jesus Christ. Where Massey has emphasized Jesus in terms of classical sin/salvation themes and Proctor has emphasized Jesus as a moral teacher and exemplar, Mitchell emphasizes Jesus' ministry of compassionate love as a witness of God's divine message. Mitchell's early work makes use of transactional analysis categories from the therapeutic work of psychology and claims that the good news of the gospel is that "God is okay, and life is okay."

---

[4]Ibid., 36.

[5]Henry H. Mitchell, *Celebration and Experience in Preaching* (Nashville: Abingdon Press, 1993), 150.

[6]Ibid., 63.

Mitchell also associates this positive theology and anthropology with African traditional religions, which some scholars consider to be more holistic and optimistic.[7] Mitchell is the first of the African American homileticians to make explicit connections to pre-slavery African religions. In *Black Preaching* he writes:

> Christianity as believed and practiced by African culture Blacks in America became a much different thing from what the whites had in mind for themselves. The intensity of Black faith and the rapid spread of Christianity among Blacks were due in part to the fact that their deeply spiritual world view had not been contaminated by white rationalism and materialistic manipulation.[8]

Mitchell develops his Afrocentric homiletic grounded on a "God-trusting world view" that he believes is common to African traditional religions and to biblical faith. His early work draws almost exclusively from Afrocentric sources (African traditional religions and black sermons, songs, and writings) while his later work broadens the influence to include the white evangelical tradition as well. Still, he never relinquishes his claim that the good news at its best affirms the goodness of God, the goodness of creation, and the worth of human beings. We will explore later how this understanding of good news operates with regard to the purpose of preaching.

Relationship between Preaching and Scripture

Mitchell's approach to preaching from the Bible is also somewhat different from the claims of earlier African American homileticians (except perhaps Taylor's). Mitchell clearly expects that preachers will preach from the Bible, saying that the Bible is authoritative within African American communities. Notice that Mitchell doesn't ground his claims on the authority of the scriptures themselves, but on the way they function within the community. "The literal, impersonal use of the scriptures would be foreign to his [*sic*] mind and spirit. The Black preacher is more likely to think of the Bible as an inexhaustible source of good preaching material than as an inert doctrinal and ethical

---

[7] The idea of Afrocentricity has come into debate within the African American scholarly community, along with specific claims about African traditional religions as they were practiced during slave-trade eras.

[8] Henry M. Mitchell, *Black Preaching* (Philadelphia and New York: J. B. Lippincott, 1970; New York: Harper & Row, 1979), 34.

authority."[9] Mitchell continues this trajectory by rejecting the reductionistic notion that the Bible is to be taken as a historically objective "textbook," even though it is full of religious truth. The Bible is a book of life, a record of timeless religious solutions to questions of faith.

Mitchell's approach to the Bible changes little over the thirty years of his scholarship. He sees it as a record of an oral tradition, a set of religious stories that can be approached not only theologically but from the perspective of literary/critical interpretation. Without being explicit about the connection, Mitchell's understanding of the preacher telling the biblical stories is very similar to the role of African storytellers who maintain a shared communal identity by the creative telling of the community's formative origins, characters, and plots. "Every storytelling preacher needs to know the meaning and purpose of the tales told, and to be sure that the focus is within the will of God for the uses of the gospel."[10] Again, Mitchell's nuance could be easily overlooked. The purpose of preaching from the Bible is not so much derived from the status of scripture as it is from the purpose to which preaching intends: "winning souls to Christ, helping them to grow, and motivating them to serve." Preachers preach from the Bible for theological purposes and within theological intentions consistent with the gospel of God's love.

His literary approach allows him to identify a moderate approach that respects the scriptures as the community's story without reducing the Bible to an object of worship itself. The assumptions about the Bible as literature also prompt him to explore the way different literary genres function, not only in the biblical texts, but in sermons as well. In *Celebration and Experience in Preaching,* Mitchell develops homiletic genres: the narrative sermon, the character sketch, the group study, and a category that includes metaphors, similes, analogs, parables, and sayings.

Relationship between the Testaments

Mitchell's claims about scripture as a whole allow him to treat both testaments as authoritative, since he sees the same God working redemptively in both. He rarely (if ever) makes claims for the ontological uniqueness of Jesus or for the superiority of Christianity over Judaism, and more frequently opts for a continuity between the testaments and the continuity of Jesus with the prophetic tradition. His normative process of evaluating the religious truth of a story or claim is its

---

[9]Ibid., 113.
[10]Mitchell, *Celebration and Experience in Preaching,* 41.

conformity with the positive aspect of a benevolent God who loves all creation.

Because Mitchell is not primarily concerned with issues of sin and depravity, he doesn't have to make traditional claims about the "special" revelation in Jesus Christ, or of his substitutionary sacrifice. This is not to say that Mitchell has anything other than a traditional christology, but he doesn't have to base his arguments on the superiority of Jesus. In fact, Mitchell tends to regularly point to the humility of Jesus and his experiences of being in solidarity with those who are oppressed. One of his published sermons, "Bethlehem Revisited: or On Starting From the Bottom" avoids a more traditional "special incarnation" gambit to argue that God is doing in Jesus what God has regularly been doing, saving folks from the bottom up.[11]

The Purpose of Preaching

Henry Mitchell has claimed that the emotional appeal of African American preaching is its fundamental strength. In one of his earliest works, Mitchell took white preachers to task for "the failure to develop a definitive response to emotion."[12] Mitchell claimed that the white homiletic tradition was captive to Western notions of rationalism that had committed a gnostic mind/body split. Such an approach overemphasized the intellectual dimension of human experience and failed to address whole persons. African American religion, by virtue of African antecedents, had developed a more holistic approach that was equipped to deal with the nonrational aspects of human experience.

The nonrational aspect of most concern to Mitchell was (and is) the dimension of emotion. Drawing on the work of John Mbiti on African "primitive" spirituality; on the work of Jung and the collective unconscious; and the insights of transactional analysis and the unconscious scripting of human experience, Mitchell proposed an approach to preach to the "transconscious" dimension of human experience. The transconscious, says Mitchell, is a kind of mystical religious integrating center that gives continuity between the sectors of human experience.[13] This nonrational dimension of religious insight is the holistic integrator of all experience, and the target of African American preaching.

---

[11]Ibid., 122–24.
[12]Henry H. Mitchell, *The Recovery of Preaching* (San Francisco: Harper & Row, 1977), 13.
[13]Ibid., 16.

Mitchell's approach is certainly consistent with Jonathan Edwards's understanding of the religious affections, with William James's psychology of religious experience, and with popular psychology strategies of the early 1970s. As Mitchell understands it, we internalize and operate from self-images that are reinforced by emotional experience. Mitchell claims that the emotional "excesses" of ecstatic African religion had reinforced an African script among the slaves.[14] The reinforced script embraced a positive African anthropology where "God's okay," "I'm okay," and "You're okay too."[15] Mitchell operates from a psychological model supported by evangelical piety and existential philosophy, but based more explicitly on the system of "core beliefs" developed in *Soul Theology*. Core beliefs

> are the bedrock attitudes that govern all deliberate behavior and relationships and also all spontaneous responses to crises…They have been acquired through life experiences, worship, and cultural exposure, and they can be altered likewise. Core beliefs are not mere propositions to which assent is given. They are the ways one trusts or fails to trust.[16]

Core beliefs are culturally shared attitudes, values, modes of behavior, and orientations toward life that characterize certain sociocultural groups. Mitchell and Cooper-Lewter claim that they are looser than creeds, but bear what we might call folk theology or folk belief. Core beliefs are borne in spirituals and blues, in folklore, in sayings and proverbs.[17] The core beliefs Mitchell and Cooper-Lewter identify

---

[14]Mitchell's work depends heavily on the idea of African "retentions," or those beliefs and behaviors that remained intact among Africans in the American diaspora. The history of scholarship regarding African retentions is not without controversy. Readers interested in pursuing this history should become familiar with the origins of the debate represented by E. Franklin Frazier, *The Negro Church in America* (New York: Schocken Books, 1963), and Melville Herskovits, *The Myth of the Negro Past* (Boston: Beacon Press, 1958). Frazier argues that the slaves had been stripped of all cultural memory by the second or third generation of slavery. Herskovits argues that certain ritual behaviors were retained throughout the generations and adapted to American forms of religious behavior. Mitchell's position is more sympathetic to Herskovits's theory.

[15]Mitchell, *The Recovery of Preaching*, 17.

[16]Henry H. Mitchell and Nicholas C. Cooper-Lewter, *Soul Theology: The Heart of American Black Culture* (San Francisco: Harper & Row, 1986), 3.

[17]Much of Teresa Fry Brown's work in *God Don't Like Ugly: African American Women Handing on Spiritual Values* (Nashville: Abingdon Press, 2000) explores the way values and attitudes are shaped by African American women. She does not seem to make explicit use of Mitchell and Cooper-Lewter's terminology, but could be interpreted as referring to a similar cultural phenomenon. See chapter 7 of this book, "African American Women and Womanists."

are the providence of God, the justice of God, the majesty and omnipotence of God, the goodness of God and the creation, the grace of God, the equality of persons, the uniqueness of persons, the family of God and humanity, and the perseverance of persons.[18]

Mitchell also makes claims for the liberation content of African American preaching. "The genius for celebration is partly responsible for the fact that enslaved and otherwise oppressed Blacks have survived the seemingly unbearable."[19] The emotional and psychological experience of radical grace reaffirms personhood. This reaffirmation of personal worth reverses the old psychological script of worthlessness, replacing it with a new script that is "well cut by the etching agent of ecstasy."[20] Mitchell claims that the presence of God is both experienced and reinforced by celebrative ecstasy, and that this personal reintegration is the foundation and motivation for liberation activity. The emotional feeling of grace-as-celebration is projected outward onto humanity as feelings of love.

> However much the details seem intellectually important, they gain their spiritual impact primarily from the way they move the hearer toward feelings of bonding with protagonists and problems, and potentials, to the end of growth for the hearer toward newness in Christ.[21]

Mitchell claims that sermonic emotion generates feelings of love toward others. That is, our own *feelings* of love and celebration will generate *activities* of love and celebration. The homiletic strategy is to generate feeling so that folks will continue to act out of that experience of ecstatic celebration. This approach is what Mervyn Warren identifies as the "effects-style" homiletic, and characterizes it as common among African American preachers.

---

[18]The categories referring to God and God's activity are quite similar to LaRue's discussion of the theological keys to biblical interpretation. See Cleophus J. LaRue, *The Heart of Black Preaching* (Louisville: Westminster John Knox Press, 2000), 25–27.

[19]Mitchell, *The Recovery of Preaching*, 54.

[20]Ibid., 55.

[21]Mitchell, *Celebration and Experience in Preaching*, 34. His arguments are similar to the Wimberlys' arguments about the psychology of personal salvation and liberation. See Anne Streaty Wimberly and Edward P. Wimberly's *Liberation and Human Wholeness: The Conversion Experiences of Black People in Slavery and Freedom* (Nashville: Abingdon Press, 1986).

Nature and Purpose of Faith Communities

Mitchell's assumptions about the purpose of preaching indicate that the church is that community of believers who come together for praise, healing, conversion, and affirmation. His emphasis on the personal and emotional dimensions is consistent with evangelical models of individual decision and motivation. While we could argue that motivating a group of individuals is the same as group motivation, Mitchell himself distinguishes between these approaches, indicating that he is primarily speaking to the inner experiences of individuals. His use of therapeutic models suggests that he sees the church as a collection of people who need to have their personal scripts rewritten so that they will trust God and celebrate divine goodness. He also assumes that this personal experience will reorient the individual more lovingly toward himself or herself and toward neighbors. This assumption is highlighted by the fact that Mitchell explicitly advocates a particular homiletic form (the group study) for motivating groups.

Mitchell's implicit ecclesiology is strongly evangelistic and oriented toward personal spirituality, but is probably most aptly characterized as a sanctuary model, where the believers come for relief from the rigors (or "slings and arrows") of daily life. Because his homiletic is self-consciously African American, his focus is dominated by the sociopolitical realities affecting African American life: oppression, second-class citizenship, and poor self-esteem. This domain of experience is what LaRue has characterized as "care of the soul," which focuses on the well-being of individuals, renewal of life, and restoring people to wholeness. "The preaching that grows out of this domain concerns itself with the healing, sustaining, guiding, and reconciling of persons as they face the changes and challenges of common human experiences, experiences that are exacerbated in black life through systemic and capricious discrimination and prejudice."[22]

Mitchell is quick to point out that such preaching is not necessarily escapist or world-denying. Just because sermons should not exhort or criticize does not mean they lack prophetic edge. "The preacher who is dominantly negative in the prophetic role should be warned that this leaves very little priestly potential for healing and empowerment."[23] Mitchell claims that celebration will empower and motivate, and that prophetic ministry emerges from positive motivation rather than the negative.

---

[22]LaRue, *The Heart of Black Preaching,* 22.
[23]Mitchell, *Celebration and Experience in Preaching,* 62.

One aspect of Mitchell's work that might easily be overlooked is his insistence that every sermon have a behavioral purpose. While every sermon should celebrate, every celebration has its own behavioral purpose that "should embody the action demanded by the biblical text...[t]he challenge is to convert a negative motivating idea to a positive behavioral purpose that flows out of the text."[24] Mitchell clearly thinks the African American church has a prophetic ministry to carry out, whether by individuals or by collective action. In an early work he wrote that "the Black preacher must also give the certain sound that helps by mobilizing the Black Church as the largest and most stable of all Black Power bases."[25] However, it's clearer in his more recent work that the most critical function of the African American Church is directed to benefit the African American community in its reclamation of dignity, racial pride, and healthy self-esteem, since "persons can rise to the level of self-giving love only after they have accepted enough of God's love to feel secure in giving."[26]

Preaching and Liturgy

Mitchell's claims about celebration would put him in a good position to associate preaching with the celebration of the eucharist, or to associate preaching with ritual formation through shared experience. However, there are few references to either one of these. In *Black Preaching,* Mitchell does make a passing reference to the high liturgical practice of priests "celebrating" the mass, but the comment is more of a justification for his own claims about celebration than a sustained consideration of how preaching and the eucharist, or Lord's supper, might inform each other.[27]

Some will also note that Mitchell's insistence on a sermon form that intentionally escalates toward ecstasy is actually an implicit recognition of ritual form. Ritual theory claims that people are "caught up" in ritual behavior, which not only unifies a group in shared understanding but orients the group toward certain types of behavior that are "rehearsed" in the ritual act itself. Mitchell writes that "people *do* what they *celebrate*," but claims that emotion is what motivates rather than the actual ritual "rehearsal" of celebration itself.

---

[24]Ibid., 53.
[25]Mitchell, *Black Preaching,* 208.
[26]Mitchell and Thomas, *Preaching for Black Self-Esteem,* 37.
[27]Mitchell, *Black Preaching,* 209.

Evans Crawford, who teaches homiletics at Howard University in Washington, D. C., takes a tack similar to other folk preaching theorists by claiming that the musical style of African American preaching is what makes it distinctive.[28] He discusses African American preaching almost entirely in terms of musical delivery. He is attempting to demonstrate that the distinctiveness of African American preaching is the genius of combining the universal appeal of musicality with an ecclesiology. Put simply, Crawford seems to be claiming that the congregation that keeps the beat together hits the street together.

Crawford is making a peculiar form of the ritual behavior argument: common activity bonds people together.[29] Most of Crawford's attention is directed to ritual behavior itself and not to any meaning of the behavior. It is one thing to say that ritual behavior binds groups together, but another to say that a particular ritual activity generates understandings that the group holds in common. When we break bread together, we engage in a ritual that has a certain horizon of theological meaning. As we perform the activity, we participate in the shared meaning of the activity. Call and response probably *is* group-building ritual behavior, but Crawford doesn't elaborate on its shared theological meaning.[30]

Mitchell, with his strong theological claims about celebration, would be in an excellent position to combine his claim of ecstatic reinforcement with claims of ritually reinforced meaning and behavior. To the contrary, Mitchell eschews discussion of ritual form with regard to African American worship, claiming that the mark of authentic

---

[28]Evans E. Crawford and Thomas Troeger, *The Hum: Call and Response in African American Preaching* (Nashville: Abingdon Press, 1995). A similar approach is in Jon Michael Spenser, comp., *Sacred Symphony: The Chanted Sermon of the Black Preacher* (Westport, Conn.: Greenwood Press, 1987); and in Gerald L. Davis, *I Got the Word in Me and I Can Sing It, You Know: A Study of the Performed African-American Sermon* (Philadelphia: University of Pennsylvania Press, 1985). All three African American scholars use Bruce Rosenberg, *The Art of the American Folk Preacher* (New York: Oxford University Press, 1970).

[29]Readers interested in pursuing work in ritual studies should begin with Mary Douglas, *Purity and Danger* (London: Routledge and Kegan Paul, 1966); Victor Turner, *Ritual Process: Structure and Anti-Structure* (New York: Aldine de Gruyter, 1995); Tom F. Driver, *The Magic of Ritual: Our Need for Liberating Rites That Transform Our Lives and Our Communities* (New York: HarperCollins, 1991); and Catherine Bell, *Ritual Theory, Ritual Practice* (New York: Oxford University Press, 1992).

[30]Crawford, *The Hum*, 32–35. Some will be resistant to the idea of ritual behavior theories in any form and will no doubt want to agree with Mitchell that certain types of participation are spontaneous. While I would not want to argue that call and response is rigidly prescribed behavior, it is ritual behavior in the sense that it is fairly predictable, occurs at certain points and not at others, has certain cues, and has parameters of appropriateness. It is possible to do it "wrong," which meets minimum requirements for it to be considered ritual behavior. The advantage of being a white outsider is the realization that call and response, along with appropriately timed clapping, is learned behavior.

African American worship is its freedom from formalism, or its jazzlike improvisation and spontaneity.[31]

Preaching and Language Studies

One of Mitchell's most significant contributions to African American homiletic theory is his insistence that preachers use common language and ordinary vernacular. Proctor, Taylor, and Massey all exhibit slightly more of what I characterize as the "gentleman's style." Of these three, Taylor's language is the grandest and most poetic, but Massey is not far behind. Proctor's style, while more plain, still bears the imprint of education and attention to standard (white) grammar. Forbes is more likely to vary his style, using a grand style for some portions of the sermon and a more vernacular style in others. Proctor occasionally traffics in vernacular, but stays mostly with his direct and plain style. Taylor, Massey, and Proctor seem to be more sympathetic to an era when the preacher was possibly the most educated person in the community and considered it a serious responsibility to model the best in all things, including standard English.

Mitchell's commitments to the community are as strong, but of a different character. Mitchell's homiletic depends on the congregation's identifying with the preacher and the sermon, and he claims that such identification cannot occur unless it is expressed in the most familiar language. He is not as interested in bringing the hearers to where he is, "uplifting" them so to speak, as he is in meeting them where they are. He insists on concrete, everyday language, concrete everyday illustrations, taken from familiar experiences of African American life. Where Taylor might not hesitate to talk about Brahms or Mozart or the great philosophers of the Western tradition, Mitchell talks about Boy Scouts, popular movies, nappy hair, domestic workers, and race riots.

Mitchell grounds his choices on his understanding of the incarnation and the *imago dei.* "No Black man," he writes, "can truly identify with a God who speaks only the language of the white oppressor. A Black rendition of scripture does in language what a Black Christ or a black Madonna does in art. God is divested of his 'proper,' white, socially distant role, a personification of deity completely outside Black culture and life."[32]

---

[31]Mitchell, *Black Preaching,* 198. Readers should note an inconsistency in Mitchell's approach. On the one hand he argues for a contextually bound African American homiletic "expectation," but on the other he argues for spontaneity. When we *expect* spontaneity, we might ask how spontaneous it is.

[32]Ibid., 155.

Mitchell claims that the African American preaching tradition uses narrative and imaginative language in a distinctive way. He has a strong appreciation for narrative memory, oral tradition, common or vernacular language, and poetic expression. Although he recommends these as poetic alternatives to abstract language because they engage the emotions, he nonetheless appreciates poetic and imaginative language as essential to the African American tradition. Mitchell encourages preachers to be more aware of images and illustrations, because they make the theological claims "come alive." He, too, appreciates the work of Gerhard Ebeling, and has employed Ebeling's characterization of faith as "an acoustical event" where God is present. In *Black Preaching,* Mitchell quotes Ebeling approvingly:

> The word of God must be left free to assert itself in an unflinchingly critical manner against distortions and fixations...theology and preaching should be free to make a translation into whatever language is required at the moment and to refuse to be satisfied with correct, archaizing repetitions of "pure doctrine."[33]

Mitchell is also aware of the critical importance of metaphor and image. In a recent work, Mitchell devotes a final brief chapter to "Metaphors, Similes, and Analogs," citing the work of Sallie McFague and one article by Paul Ricoeur to discuss the epistemic nature of metaphor.[34] While Ricoeur's heavily Freudian work might be interpreted to support Mitchell's emotive theories, it is not as clear that McFague's work lends itself in the way Mitchell appropriates it. Ricoeur and McFague are probably both making assumptions about theological imagination rather than ecstatic reinforcement. Ricouer and McFague discuss imagination as "the holding of a concrete image in the mind" and distinguish it from either intellectualizing (which is abstract and not concrete) or from emotion, which deals with somatic responses. It is the case that both McFague and Ricouer disparage abstract propositional

---

[33]Gerhard Ebeling, *Word and Faith,* trans. James W. Leitch (Philadelphia: Fortress Press, 1963), 9, 11; cited in Mitchell, *Black Preaching,* 25. Readers should note that Fred Craddock's watershed book in homiletic theory, *As One Without Authority* (Enid, Okla.: Phillips University Press, 1971), was published a year *later* than Mitchell's *Black Preaching.* David James Randolph, *The Renewal of Preaching: A New Homiletic Based on the New Hermeneutic* (Philadelphia: Fortress Press) was published in 1969, when *Black Preaching* was most likely in the process of publication.

[34] In Mitchell, *Celebration and Experience in Preaching,* 139–43.

language, as does Mitchell.[35] Neither Ricouer nor McFague would consider imagination a particularly "cognitive" activity even though it does occur in the mind, or more accurately, in the "mind's eye." To use my earlier example, I might imagine a woman slitting a man's throat, because of someone else's use of particular words. I could analyze it, intellectualize it, abstract ideas from it, and call it "murder." Or I could have an emotional response to it that might be called fear or anger, depending on my perspective. It's not clear from Mitchell's work whether imagination (the holding of images in the mind) is a function of the emotive, the intuitive, or the cognitive consciousness.

Homiletic Method

As we might expect, Mitchell's method for putting a sermon together is more oriented toward the hearers than toward the text itself. The text provides theological or religious truth that is to be "grasped" by the hearers in some behaviorally specific way. After choosing a text, the preacher must determine the behavioral purpose of the text so that the sermon can serve the behavioral purpose. While *textual* considerations are important, African American *contextual* considerations ultimately shape the sermon toward the specific behavioral purposes and the particular form of celebration. Mitchell requires that every sermon end with celebration, moving toward a crescendo of emotional expression. He refers to this overall homiletic structure as the "logic of the emotions."

Beyond the demand that each sermon ends with a celebrative climax, Mitchell also urges that sermons be formed in what David Buttrick calls "moves." A sermon is composed of four or five major units of thought, each one having its own characteristics and quality, or what Buttrick refers to as "point-of-view." Buttrick's "move" method is not the same as the older "point-making sermon" where ideas are abstracted from a text for objective or exegetical consideration. Rather, the moves follow the major narrative episodes or the major rhetorical shifts in a text. Mitchell's appropriation of Buttrick's method is somewhat different, since Mitchell insists that behavioral purpose, not internal textual "logic" or textual structure, drives the sermon structure. Mitchell uses the language of Buttrick's homiletic without following some of its basic

---

[35]See McFague's discussion of imagination and language, along with her appropriation of Ricoeur, in Sallie McFague, *Metaphorical Theology: Models of God in Religious Language* (Philadelphia: Fortress Press, 1982).

mandates.[36] Mitchell still tends to distill points or propositions and shape them into coherent and distinct sections, which is not surprising since his propositionally stated behavioral purpose is the main driving force of the sermon.[37]

The overall move structure and the mandate to end with celebration are the only hard-and-fast homiletical rules for Mitchell. Beyond those considerations, preachers may assume a great deal of freedom in the sermon form or sermon genre they select. Mitchell, unlike Taylor, does not suggest that sermon structure takes its cues from the text structure or literary genre of the text. Mitchell identifies several sermon genres and discusses each one in brief sections. The *narrative-type* sermon may be either an extended and expanded retelling of the biblical story in the mode of Clarence Jordan's *Cotton Patch Gospels,* or it may be a series of movelike vignettes with a little story illustration in each section. The *character-sketch* sermon is built around a particular biblical character who may serve as a moral exemplar and may draw from a variety of texts. One character sketch sermon featuring the apostle Paul is only loosely text-driven, and actually makes reference to a number of epistolary phrases. The *group study* sermon genre mentioned earlier is a sustained focus on biblical understandings of particular groups, whether of women, parents, marginalized folks, teenagers, or men, for example. The behavioral purpose of a group study sermon is to address the shared group identity of the auditors, usually for the purpose of group cohesion and inspiration. Mitchell also discusses a genre that he calls *stream-of-consciousness,* but doesn't give examples or parameters for sermons in this mode.

He *does* insist that language be accessible and that preachers use concrete, familiar, and metaphorical language. As we noted in an earlier section, Mitchell does not consider metaphor and other figures of speech to be simple ornamentation, but generally discusses them in relation to their emotive power.

Mitchell uses personal anecdote extensively, frequently draws on African folklore or African American common wisdom, illustrates with other biblical stories and characters, and encourages the use of inspiring

---

[36]Mitchell regularly includes exegetical and historical details that Buttrick would eschew, and Mitchell may succeed more at taking the congregation back in history than in making the theological claims immediately relevant. See David Buttrick, *Homiletic: Moves and Structures* (Philadelphia: Fortress Press, 1987).

[37]Mitchell, *Celebration and Experience in Preaching,* 74–75. Mitchell offers a worksheet for sermon preparation. See also Martha J. Simmons and Henry H. Mitchell, "A Study-Guide to Accompany *Celebration and Experience in Preaching*" (self-published, 1993).

poetry and hymns (especially during the celebrative climax). He rarely uses illustrations from the world of the arts or literature, though he occasionally uses illustrations from the worlds of science, psychology, or sociology. Because of his theological commitments to the African American community, racial themes are common, and (unlike Proctor) he rarely mentions white individuals or groups in an intentionally positive way. He is the most thoroughly Afrocentric homiletician we have considered so far.

Henry Mitchell is without a doubt the premier African American academic homiletician of the twentieth century. He has read more deeply and integrated more work from other disciplines than any homiletician in our modest survey. James Massey has perhaps taught and written more extensively, but no one in the African American homiletic guild has integrated a more diverse variety of scholarship than Henry Mitchell. Invariably, when contemporary African American preachers and theology students make claims about the African American pulpit, they do so informed by the work of Henry Mitchell.[38]

---

[38]See Cleophus LaRue's opening comments on Henry Mitchell in *The Heart of Black Preaching*, 10.

7

African American Women and Womanists

African American women have been preaching justice for centuries. They have preached on street corners, in prisons, by sickbeds, in schools, in small groups, in women's Bible studies, in churches, in homes, and any place they could say a word for God.[1]

It should come as no surprise that a theological discipline as traditionally male-dominated as homiletics (along with its obvious relationship to the male-dominated pulpit) would be among the last of the disciplines to reflect the intellectual and social concerns of African American female academics. Within the world of Eurocentric homiletic theory, women scholars are just beginning to gain access to the rhetorical space. In the twentieth century, the first book written from a self-consciously female perspective was *Weaving the Sermon,* by white feminist

[1]Teresa L. Fry Brown, "An African American Woman's Perspective: Renovating Sorrow's Kitchen," in *Preaching Justice: Ethnic and Cultural Perspectives,* ed. Christine M. Smith (Cleveland: United Church Press, 1998), 57.

Christine M. Smith, in 1989.[2] Ella Mitchell had written brief comments in the introduction to her first edited volume of women's sermons, and Elizabeth Achtemeier, a white Hebrew Bible scholar had written a brief volume on creative preaching. Fourteen years have elapsed since Smith's book. Since African American women have had more obstacles to education and to publication than white men, African American men, or white women, it's no surprise that there is currently no extensive scholarship on homiletics by African American women. There *are* perspectives emerging, however, and the contours of African American women's homiletic concerns are coming into view.

A word is in order about this project and the authorial decision to attend first to the senior male "experts" and to leave the women until the end. This approach is frequently criticized, and for good reason. To begin with, separating the women from the men reinforces or reinscribes the whole notion of gender difference, which can be intellectually problematic, especially as it moves toward any kind of biological essentialism. In particular we might want to undercut the popular notion that there is some general "feminine" or "female" approach to preaching that can be identified and studied.

The other problem is creating the impression that the women are somehow inferior or parenthetical to the male figures. The women we'll survey in this chapter are relatively new voices; there are almost no senior female homileticians. Our trajectory up to this point has been roughly chronological. The point of leaving the women homileticians until the end is, in one way, simply chronologically accurate. The strategy of dealing with them in one chapter is likewise practical, because there is hardly enough material on any one woman to sustain more than a long section.

But the decision to treat the women at the end of this project is also theological, or somewhat proleptic. I would claim that the insights of African American female homileticians will shape the future of homiletics, both black and white, male and female, in ways that are yet to be discerned. Rather than see the women as a "footnote" to the male

---

[2]This assertion might be disputed by some who would want to claim Elizabeth Achtemeier's *Creative Preaching: Finding the Words* (Nashville: Abingdon Press, 1980) as the first. I am inclined to discount Achtemeier's book, primarily geared toward parish preachers and not toward the academy, as a biblical exegetical "help" and not engaged in theoretical or women's issues. Even if we grant Achtemeier priority, that in itself is telling, since Achtemeier is by admission not a feminist but a traditional (and somewhat conservative) biblical scholar. In the first chapter of her book, Smith comments on the absence of theoretical work by women homileticians, citing as exceptions the introductory comments of Ella Mitchell in the first volume of *Those Preachin' Women* (Valley Forge, Pa.: Judson Press, 1985). See Christine M. Smith, *Weaving the Sermon: Preaching in a Feminist Perspective* (Louisville: Westminster/John Knox Press, 1989), 13.

homileticians, it is more appropriate to see them as the direction of the future. The women are last because they have been the last on the scene, and this renders them the wave of the future, prophetesses who will point the way.

Ella Pearson Mitchell

The Rev. Dr. Ella Pearson Mitchell is in a unique category as a teacher of preachers and an advocate for women who has written very little. Ella Mitchell has devoted most of her publications to sermon collections. Her approach to homiletic theory has surfaced primarily in introductory material for the three sermon collections she edited, as well as in her coauthored work with Henry Mitchell, *Together for Good: Lessons from Fifty-Five Years of Marriage,* which chronicles the Mitchells' life of ministry together. She is to be commended for her efforts to render women's preaching more visible and part of the official record. Her 1991 publication of *To Preach or Not To Preach: 21 Outstanding Black Preachers Say Yes!* solicited the support of male and female clergy in advocating for women in the pulpit.

Ella P. Mitchell is a teacher, preacher, and outstanding churchwoman from Atlanta, Georgia. Born in Charleston, South Carolina, in 1917, Ella Pearson began preaching and serving the church in 1935 when her father, Pastor Joseph Richard Pearson, allowed her to conduct vesper and prayer services.[3] "He would let me preach when I came home from college, and I used to do the sermons for chapel at Talladega College. Joel Nichols, the Dean of the Chapel at Talladega, would allow me to do them because I was the only one majoring in the field of religion."[4]

Mitchell entered Union Theological Seminary in New York City in 1941 and subsequently met her husband, Henry H. Mitchell, with whom she has ministered for more than fifty years. At Union, she didn't pursue a Master of Divinity degree, since that was "not what women did" at that time.[5] She recounts that it was difficult for her to even get into seminary at first. "When I tried to get into the New England schools (Yale and Harvard) for seminary, they told me to try

---

[3] Martha J. Simmons, "An Interview with Ella Pearson Mitchell," *The African American Pulpit* 3, no. 4 (Fall 2000): 91.

[4] Simmons, "An Interview with Ella Mitchell," 91.

[5] Ibid. Mitchell claims that she was steered into Christian education on the advice of the dean, who insisted that the women were there to find husbands. "I never considered the pastorate because no one steered me in that direction," Mitchell says.

other schools. They did me a favor; I tried Union, and that was the place."[6]
She graduated in 1943 with an M.A. from the Christian education
program and has been supportive of women in ministry her whole career,
even though she struggled for decades with her own call to ministry.
She earned a D.Min. from The School of Theology at Claremont in
1974 and was ordained in 1978, at Allen Temple in Oakland, more than
three decades after completing her theological studies at Union.[7]

Ella Mitchell was associate professor of Christian education and
director of continuing education at Virginia Union Seminary when her
husband was dean, 1982–1986. Ella and Henry Mitchell are co-mentors
in the Doctor of Ministry Program at United Theological Seminary in
Dayton, Ohio, and were founders of the Ecumenical Center for Black
Church Studies in Los Angeles. Dr. Ella Mitchell was the first woman
dean of Sisters Chapel at Spelman College and also taught at the
American Baptist Seminary of the West and the School of Theology at
Claremont. She and Henry Mitchell co-taught homiletics from 1988 to
1995 at Interdenominational Theological Center, a consortium of
theological schools committed to African American ministries. Dr. Ella
Mitchell is the editor of three volumes in the series *Those Preaching
Women;* editor of *Women: To Preach or Not to Preach;* and coauthor of a
joint autobiography, *Together for Good: Lessons from Fifty-Five Years of
Marriage* with husband Henry H. Mitchell. In 2000, Henry and Ella
Mitchell were copresidents of the Academy of Homiletics, the primary
professional guild for those who teach and research homiletics.

Ella Pearson Mitchell understands the obstacles to women in the
pulpit and encourages women *first* to be sure of their call and then to
be prepared to wait without forcing the situation.[8] She herself has
followed this strategy, preaching from the floor when denied access to
the pulpit.

Mitchell makes more than one reference to Jarena Lee, nineteenth-
century evangelist-at-large for the African Methodist Episcopal Church.
Reverend Richard Allen, the founder of the A.M.E. church, denied Lee
ordination on the basis of her gender:

> Rev. Richard Allen perceived that it was unjust for Blacks, free
> and slaves, to be relegated to the balcony and restricted to a

---

[6]Ibid., 93.

[7]Ella P. Mitchell and Henry H. Mitchell, *Together for Good: Lessons from Fifty-Five Years of
Marriage* (Kansas City: Andrews McMeel, 1999), 225–26. J. Alfred Smith, Sr., preached her
ordination sermon.

[8]Simmons, "An Interview with Ella Mitchell," 93.

special time to pray and kneel at the communion table; for this he should be praised. Yet because of his acceptance of the patriarchal system Allen was unable to see the injustice in relegating women to one area of the church–the pews–by withholding ordination from women.[9]

Jarena Lee's historic response is the same ground for Ella Mitchell to preach and pursue her ministry. Lee responded to Allen:

> Oh how careful ought we be, lest through our by-laws of church government and discipline, we bring into disrepute even the word of life. For as unseemly as it may appear nowadays for a woman to preach, it should be remembered that nothing is impossible with God. And why should it be thought impossible, heterodox, or improper for a woman to preach, seeing the Saviour died for the woman as well as the man?[10]

Mitchell tells the story of Lee to women pursuing ministry and Christian service of all kinds. Mitchell laughs, "She was a great preacher, but Bishop Allen never got around to ordaining her; but she was still a great preacher."[11] If African American history and culture are authoritative for Henry Mitchell, the particular history of African American women is a theological resource for Ella Mitchell. Her homiletic approach is similar to her husband's in that she insists sermons have an identifiable genre and behavioral purpose that is derived from the intention of the biblical text itself. She devotes much of her preparation to extensive exegesis and word study, but always with an eye toward those who have been rendered silent or invisible within the text. "I often look for what has been missed in a passage. Women and poor people are often missed in texts."[12] She regularly preaches about

---

[9]Jacquelyn Grant, "Black Theology and the Black Woman," in Gayraud S. Wilmore and James H. Cone, *Black Theology: A Documentary History, 1966-1979* (Maryknoll, N.Y.: Orbis Books, 1979), 424.

[10]Jacquelyn Grant, "Black Theology and the Black Woman," 425, citing Jarena Lee, *The Life and Religious Experience of Jarena Lee: A Colored Lady Giving an Account of Her Call to Preach the Gospel,* Philadelphia, 1836.

[11]Simmons, "An Interview with Ella Mitchell," 94. Mitchell also refers to the Lee story in the introduction to volume 1 of *Those Preachin' Women,* 12–13. It's interesting to note that Mitchell tells the story to argue that Lee was still a preacher in spite of Bishop Allen's reluctance to ordain her. The African American women homileticians who are newer to the scene do not share Mitchell's position of nonconfrontation. Teresa Fry Brown uses the Jarena Lee story, as do others, to highlight *not* Lee's faithfulness, but Bishop Allen's sexism.

[12]Simmons, "An Interview with Ella Mitchell," 92.

women of faith in the Bible as well as ordinary and extraordinary women of faith in African American history.

Leontine T. C. Kelly

Retired Bishop Leontine T. C. Kelly was born in 1920, in Washington, D.C. Her father was a prominent Methodist minister, and her mother was respected for being an advocate of women and the African American community. Dr. Kelly received her B.A. from Virginia Union University in 1960, and was a public school teacher for eight years before she began her career in ordained ministry. She received a master of divinity degree in 1976 from Union Theological Seminary in Richmond, Virginia, having been called to the ministry after the death of her husband, the Rev. Dr. James David Kelly, in 1969. While serving the Galilee Church in the Virginia Annual Conference, she was ordained a deacon by Bishop William R. Cannon in 1972. Kelly served in the San Francisco area from 1984 until her retirement in 1992. Bishop Kelly was ordained to the episcopacy in 1984 by the Western Jurisdictional Conference of the United Methodist Church, the second female and first African American woman to be elected bishop of any major denomination. She served as bishop of the California-Nevada Annual Conference and president of the Western Jurisdiction College of Bishops.

Kelly's career came full circle in 1988 when she retired as bishop and returned to teaching to become a visiting professor at the Pacific School of Religion in Berkeley, California. She is a past president of the AIDS National Interfaith Network (ANIN), a past president of the Inter-religious Health Care ACCESS Campaign, and currently works with Chosen Peace, which combines politics and the church to bring about effective change. Kelly holds a number of honorary degrees and awards, including The Southern Christian Leadership Conference's Grass Roots Leadership Award and the Martin Luther King, Jr., "Drum Major for Justice" Award. She also received *Ebony* magazine's Black Achievement Award and, in 1998, was the first recipient of the Bishop Leontine T.C. Kelly Justice Award, presented by the Black Clergywomen of the United Methodist Church. In October 2000, Kelly was inducted into the National Women's Hall of Fame for her contributions to American women's history in the humanities.

Recently Bishop Kelly led a peaceful protest at the United Methodist General Conference in Cleveland, in solidarity with lesbian, gay, bisexual, and transgendered persons. Bishop Kelly and others protested the conference's support for the policy that homosexuality is incompatible with Christian teaching.

Bishop Kelly published a single essay on preaching, which outlines the narrative quality of black preaching to tell of God's redemptive activity. Kelly claimed that preaching is the particular word of God to a people in need of affirmation. The particularity of black preaching, according to Kelly, is based on the biblical Israelites and their particular needs as both captive and waiting.[13] She discusses the phenomena of call and response as part of the communal nature of African American preaching. In these comments, she is not making particularly new claims for the tradition.

However, Kelly has not shied away from claiming that the African American church, like all churches, was sexist, and that this gender bias surfaces particularly around issues of preaching. Kelly claims that African American women have significant obstacles to full ministry in the African American church and have been rendered historically invisible by a history of male domination. In her critique of this gender bias, she cites Charles V. Hamilton's *The Black Preacher in America* (New York: Morrow, 1972) as an example of this exclusion, since Hamilton did not recognize any tradition of women preachers.

Her critique of sexism is grounded on the theological claim that the Creator God is creator of *all* humans and that the slave tradition of African American Christianity demanded full personhood and full humanity for all, not just for males.[14] She notes that even "illiterate" women could preach from this tradition, and that women's experience of oppression and of their liberation (through Jesus) give preaching testimonial authenticity and an anticipation of hope. Her claims about the audacity of women preaching is strongly reminiscent of the claims made by male homileticians for African American males. Kelly's approach to the issue of women preaching is somewhat more outspoken than Ella Mitchell's, but not as critical as some of the younger African American women scholars.

Kelly cites Sojourner Truth, Harriet Tubman, Mary McLeod Bethune, Nannie Burroughs, Barbara Jordan, and Shirley Chisholm as exemplars of prophetic women whose strength comes from a traditional black

---

[13]Leontine T. C. Kelly, "Preaching in the Black Tradition," in *Women Ministers,* ed. Judith L. Weidman (San Francisco: Harper & Row, 1985), 67–76.

[14]Note the "core belief" of equal personhood that Henry Mitchell and Cooper-Lewter also cite. See chapter 6 on Henry Mitchell for a discussion of the core beliefs.

preaching model. She also calls attention to the connection between preaching and social change as a natural outgrowth of theological understanding. She considers Martin Luther King, Jr., Joseph Lowery, Andrew Young, Jesse Jackson, and Benjamin Hooks to be products of the social imperatives of Christian proclamation.

The "mission context" for black preaching, according to Kelly, is in urban ministry, education, housing, and issues of unemployment. Without articulating an ecclesiology, Kelly seems to assume the primary vocation of the African American church is toward the community, not to individual selves or to be limited to the care of souls or to institutional maintenance. Preaching is prophetic, she seems to claim, and it results in social activity on behalf of the world that God so loves.

Transitions: The Emergence of Womanist Theology

Bishop Kelly and Dr. Ella P. Mitchell are featured here as forerunners of African American women's approaches to homiletic theory. Both promoted equal rights in the pulpit, even while they embraced different public approaches to advocacy. For several years, anyone studying the contributions of African American women to the recent twentieth-century pulpit had only their writings from which to draw.

In the last decade of the century, however, African American women theologians began to develop several distinctive alternatives to Western classical theology and to the approaches both of twentieth-century white feminists and of African American male religious scholars. Three of the women who provided the leadership in what would become known as womanist approaches did their doctoral work in the mid-1980s at Union Theological Seminary, where James Cone was on the faculty. Jacquelyn Grant (Ph.D., 1985), Katie Cannon (Ph.D., 1983), and Delores Williams (Ph.D., 1991) developed theological approaches influenced by Cone and Beverly Wildung Harrison, white feminist theologian and ethicist. At least one scholar has distinguished the Union womanists who studied with Cone as more dialogical than others (particularly Cheryl Sanders) with a more intentionally Afrocentric approach.[15]

Alice Walker coined the contemporary use of the adjective *womanist,* which comes from the cultural expression directed at young women

---

[15]Rufus Burrow, Jr., "Enter Womanist Theology and Ethics," *Western Journal of Black Studies* 2, no.1 (Spring 1998): 23. Burrow also discusses the Roundtable Discussion and the differences that emerged from that meeting.

"you acting womanish," which usually refers to outrageous, audacious, courageous, or willful behavior. Acting womanish means wanting to know more and in greater depth than is considered "good" for one; it can also mean "responsible" and "in charge." A womanist appreciates, values, and prefers other women, loving women, whether sexually or nonsexually. A womanist is committed to the survival and wholeness of the whole community and of entire persons. A womanist loves life in the flesh, including food, dance, and nature. Womanist is to feminist as purple is to lavender.[16] Grant, Cannon, and Williams have been key figures in the theological appropriation of Walker's definition.

Jacquelyn Grant is currently the Fuller E. Calloway Professor of systematic theology at the Interdenominational Theological Center in Atlanta. Dr. Grant earned her bachelor's degree from Bennett College in Greensboro, North Carolina, in 1970, and her Master of Divinity from the Interdenominational Theological Center's Turner Theological Seminary in 1973. She's an ordained itinerant elder in the AME Church and associate pastor of Victory AME Church in Atlanta. Grant serves on the Ecumenical Association of Third World Theologies, the Black Theology Board, the Commission on World Missions and Evangelism of the World Council of Churches, and the steering committee for Black Theology of the American Academy of Religion. In 1981, Grant founded the Black Women in Church and Society Center at ITC, and serves as its director.

Grant's first book, *White Women's Christ, Black Women's Jesus,* challenged sexism and racism in a double critique. One of Grant's strongest challenges to white feminists was in the implicit assumption that *feminist* theology spoke to and for all women. "The seriousness of the charge White feminists make regarding inappropriate male universalism is undercut by the limited perspective which presumes the universality of women's experience."[17] Grant charged white feminists with implicit racism, claiming that gender critiques did not fully attend to issues of race and class. Grant argued from a christological assumption,

---

[16]Alice Walker, *In Search of Our Mothers' Gardens: Womanist Prose* (San Diego: Harcourt Brace Jovanovich, 1983). Shawn Copeland speculates that Walker's use of the term evolves from its first use in introductory comments ("Coming Apart: By Way of Introduction to Lorde, Teish and Gardner") for an anthology on pornography–Laura Lederer, ed., *Take Back the Night: Women on Pornography* (New York: W. Morrow, 1980)–and was subsequently printed in Alice Walker, *Can't Keep a Good Woman Down* (New York: Harcourt Brace Jovanovich, 1981). See Copeland's discussion in "Christian Ethics and Theology in Womanist Perspective," *Journal of Feminist Studies in Religion* 5, no. 2 (Fall 1989): 97–102.

[17]Jacquelyn Grant, *White Women's Christ, Black Women's Jesus: Feminist Christology and Womanist Response* (Atlanta: Scholars Press, 1989), 5.

informed by the folk beliefs of ordinary African American Christian women, that since "Jesus located the Christ with the outcast, the least, christology [and implicitly, theology] must emerge out of the condition of the least."[18]

Grant found the feminist critique of patriarchy helpful, despite its limitations, to support Christian mandates for egalitarianism and a focus on shared humanity, a theme picked up by Kelly Brown Douglas in *The Black Christ*.[19] Grant argues, as Cone did, for a continuity with the prophetic tradition of the Hebrew Bible. In a shift toward an "ontology of marginality" Grant aligns her project with theologies that critique power and hierarchy of all forms. By embracing a critique of power (also a strategy of ethicist Beverly Harrison), Grant is able to analyze and expose basic church leadership structures that reinscribe the continuation of a privileged class, whether that is masculine power, white power, or class privilege.[20]

Grant's subsequent works are two volumes she edited: *Perspectives on Womanist Theology* and *The Recovery of Black Presence*.[21]

Delores S. Williams is another womanist theologian who uses a three-way critique of classical Christianity. Williams is Paul Tillich Professor of Theology and Culture at Union Theological Seminary in New York City. A native of Louisville, Kentucky, she graduated from the University of Louisville in 1965, and holds her M.A. and her Ph.D. from Union Theological Seminary. Williams was also a key figure in the "ReImagining God" movement of the mid-1990s, claiming that the language and the liturgy of the church render women invisible and need to be renarrated.

An overriding theme in Williams's work is that of "surrogacy." She claims that Jesus as a surrogate or substitute figure reinforces passivity, a problem for African American women who have shouldered the labor not only of white women, but also of African American men. "In the black community black women could be pressured by social circumstances to step into the role of head of household in lieu of

---

[18]Ibid., 6.

[19]Ibid., 220. See Kelly Brown Douglas, *The Black Christ* (Maryknoll, N.Y.: Orbis Books, 1994).

[20]See also Grant's essay on the servanthood model and its support of hierarchical structures in "The Sin of Servanthood," in *A Troubling in My Soul: Womanist Perspectives on Evil & Suffering*, ed. Emilie M. Townes (Maryknoll, N.Y.: Orbis Books, 1993), 199–216.

[21]Jacquelyn L. Grant, ed., *Perspectives on Womanist Theology*, Black Church Scholars 7 (Atlanta: ITC Press, 1995); and Randall C. Bailey and Jacquelyn L. Grant, eds., *The Recovery of Black Presence: An Interdisciplinary Exploration: Essays in Honor of Dr. Charles B. Copher* (Nashville: Abingdon Press, 1995).

absent male energy and presence."[22] The implication is that women and men have separate but complementary roles advocated by Christian theology that limits women's roles as spiritual leaders in their own right.

Instead, Williams embraces biblical images of strong women and mothers as figures of profound theological significance. Rather than focusing on suffering as a virtue, Williams reclaims childbirth and nurturing. Hers is an incarnational approach that celebrates life. Williams assumes that her approach will be problematic for some African American male theologians and pastors who have not historically challenged the gender biases promoted by the tradition or embedded in biblical theology. Ethically, what must be reclaimed and revalued is the role of strong women that does not reduce to surrogacy. In a discussion that supports Ella Mitchell's focus on the "invisible," Katie Cannon's attention to certain theoethical themes about women, and Cheryl Sanders's sustained attention to women's sermons, Williams reclaims Mary as a central figure who displaces the Hagar and mammy figures of tradition. Liberation does not come "by any means necessary," but by the life-enhancing truth contained in images of nurturing, feeding, and caring for the least of these. Her attention to images, to language, and to the way women are rendered in ordinary Christian expression have implications for homiletic theory.

The work of Cannon will be dealt with extensively in a following section, but it's critical to understand the context of womanist theology and how it challenged dominant white theological approaches as well as Black Theology and African American male scholars. Several African American women scholars in religion met in 1989 for the Roundtable Discussion called "Christian Ethics and Theology in Womanist Perspectives," during which Alice Walker's definition of womanism was discussed as a model for theological appropriation. There was not uniformity among the womanists, and some significant differences of opinion emerged. Cheryl Sanders, of the Divinity School at Howard University, strongly challenged the adequacy of a secular term for theological reflection. She also hinted that some womanist religion scholars had been coopted in their efforts by drawing on the writings of white feminist theologians, saying, "Self-hatred manifests itself as unmistakably in the academy as in the ghetto when we are pressured

---

[22]Delores S. Williams, *Sisters in the Wilderness: The Challenge of Womanist God-Talk* (Maryknoll, N.Y.: Orbis Books, 1993), 61. See also Delores S. Williams, *Black Theology in a New Key: Feminist Theology in a Different Voice* (Maryknoll, N.Y.: Orbis Books, 1996).

to employ our oppressor's criteria to evaluate our own work and worth. To see black women embracing and engaging our material is a celebration in itself."[23]

Katie Cannon apparently felt the critique was directed primarily at her appropriations of Beverly Harrison and Elisabeth Schüssler Fiorenza; Cannon had drawn on the work of white feminists more regularly than the other contributors to the Roundtable. Cannon and Williams eventually responded to the issue in print. Delores Williams wrote a 1993 essay, "Womanist/Feminist Dialogue," claiming that there were strengths and liabilities in the dialogical approach, and that tension was simply to be expected.[24] Katie Cannon argued in 1995 that drawing on a breadth of scholarship was completely appropriate and, in fact, ethically demanded. "Sanders' devaluation of credibility consequent on such a conservative framework of sources only encourages guesswork, blank spots, and time-consuming busy work, the reinvention of the proverbial wheel over and over again…Staying open-minded as heterogeneous theoreticians may prove to be the most difficult ethical challenge in securing and extending the legacy of our intellectual life."[25]

What is particularly interesting for our purposes here is to trace the ongoing influence of Cone's work as it is challenged and reinterpreted through womanist appropriations. But beyond that, it's interesting to see how womanist approaches are not uniformly consistent with either Cone's Black Theology Project, or with Henry Mitchell's claims about Afrocentricity. In addition to the faculty presence of Cone and Harrison, James Forbes was teaching homiletics at Union during the same years (1976–1989). While there is no particular reason to assume that Cannon, Grant, or Williams would have taken classes with him, it's fair to assume that his own progressive and dialogical approach to social justice preaching would have been part of the community ethos. Another reason the Roundtable Discussion is figural to womanist issues, particularly for homiletics, is that one of the key disagreements between Sanders and the other Roundtable participants was the issue of sexual identity.[26] Sanders's own theological conservatism and commitment to heterosexual intimacy and to family structures was a key factor in her

---

[23]Cheryl Sanders, "Christian Ethics and Theology in Womanist Perspective," Roundtable Discussion, 1989, 111.

[24]Delores Williams, "Womanist/Feminist Dialogue," *Journal of Feminist Studies in Religion* (Spring 1993): 67ff.

[25]Katie Cannon, "Appropriation and Reciprocity," in *Katie's Canon: Womanism and the Soul of the Black Community* (New York: Continuum, 1995), 131.

[26]Contributors to the Roundtable publication were Sanders, Cannon, Emilie M. Townes, M. Shawn Copeland, bell hooks, and Cheryl Townsend Gilkes.

rejection of Walker's definition of womanist. Her characterization of Walker's definition was that it was theologically inadequate and morally questionable.

Katie Geneva Cannon

Dr. Katie Geneva Cannon grew up in Kannapolis, North Carolina, in the Baby Boom era. She holds degrees from Barber-Scotia College and Johnson C. Smith Seminary, which is part of the Interdenominational Theological Center in Atlanta, Georgia. She was the first African American woman to be ordained to ministry within the Presbyterian Church (USA), in 1974, and she pursued doctoral studies in ethics at Union Theological Seminary. In 1983, she was the first African American woman to receive the Ph.D. at Union. She had begun her doctoral work in Hebrew Bible, but later switched to ethics.

Dr. Cannon taught at Episcopal Divinity School and at Temple University. She has taught as visiting professor at other seminaries and schools around the country. She has taken an appointment at Union Theological Seminary and Presbyterian School of Christian Education as full professor of theology and ethics in Richmond, Virginia. Among her writings are *Black Womanist Ethics* (1988), *Katie's Canon: Womanism and the Soul of the Black Community* (1995), and *Teaching Preaching: Isaac Rufus Clark and Black Sacred Rhetoric* (2002)[27]; she also is a coeditor of three volumes: *God's Fierce Whimsy: Christian Feminism and Theological Education* (1985), *Inheriting Our Mothers' Gardens: Feminist Theology in Third World Perspective* (1988), and *Interpretation for Liberation* (1989). Cannon's life story forms the opening portrait in Sara Lawrence-Lightfoot's celebrated book *I've Known Rivers: Lives of Loss and Liberation.*

Cannon's own personal history has taught her that even though women represent the majority of sermon-hearers, their experience and value are diminished by homiletical strategies that valorize male figures, masculine understandings, and masculine spirituality.

> The one place where Black men have been allowed to be men has been in the pulpit. I knew this. If I became a preacher, would I, a Black woman, be functioning as a castrator in collusion with the oppressor? Would I harm Black men?...I still had to grapple with my own socialization, images of women evangelists in long

---

[27]Cannon's book was just going to press as this volume was in revision. My discussion doesn't reflect Cannon's new work on preaching.

skirts, all dressed in white–pure, above sin, sanctified. It wasn't me. I never saw myself as a pastor–perhaps because so many field-education opportunities were closed to me as a woman. When I passed my ordination exams in the Presbyterian church, they didn't know what to do with me. I felt like E.T.[28]

Feeling out of place was not new for Cannon, who felt like she didn't fit in even at Barber-Scotia, an all-women's college just seven miles from her hometown. She felt most at home at ITC, but even there she was among a handful of women in her incoming class, temporarily housed in "guest rooms" while the school tried to figure out what on earth to do with them. Her male colleagues supported her call to ministry, affirmed her gifts, and encouraged her to preach. "The harvest is plentiful, laborers few. Who are we to stop you if God has called you to this ministry?"[29] Later at Union, out of her Southern context and in a Northern seminary where all her colleagues, black and white, came from middle and upper classes ("elite" in her eyes), she would feel alien again. To her surprise and frustration, her African American male classmates at Union were openly hostile to women in ministry. In addition to all the conflicted loyalties she already experienced, there was the additional conflict between race and gender.[30] The contrasts would continue to form her, to give her a certain ease she had never imagined possible, but also thrusting her into an academic and professional life marked by the ambiguities of race, gender, and class.

Even though her advanced studies were not in the area of homiletics, Cannon has lectured and written in the area and is frequently called on to preach. She is not, strictly speaking, a homiletician, but her work with Elisabeth Schüssler Fiorenza's rhetorical critical approach to biblical texts has produced work of significant homiletical importance. In "Womanist Interpretation and Preaching in the Black Church," Cannon appropriates Schüssler Fiorenza's argument about rhetorical situations and the function of language to create a world. Cannon connects this directly to the orality of the African American tradition, to the presentation of ancestors, and to claims of emancipatory praxis. She is interested in analyzing the methodology of her own preaching

---

[28]Dee Dee Risher, "Giving Forward: An Interview with Katie Geneva Cannon," *The Other Side* (March-April 1997): 28. For more personal accounts of Cannon's ongoing dilemma with sexism, racism, and classism, see the narratives in Sara Lawrence-Lightfoot, *I've Known Rivers: Lives of Loss and Liberation* (Reading, Mass.: Addison-Wesley, 1994).

[29]Risher, "Giving Forward," 28.

[30]Lightfoot, *I've Known Rivers,* 106–7.

instructor Isaac R. Clark to demonstrate "why certain theoethical themes and motifs are present and others absent."[31]

Cannon makes strong claims for the hearers' "imaginative response" and a rhetorical strategy that works "inside the mind." Without discounting the emotional dimension of preaching, she wants to focus attention on the way rhetorical strategies within sermons tend to privilege certain groups and interpretive strategies, along with certain ethical values. Cannon claims that the sermon calls into question "the social network of power/knowledge relations," that the sermon reveals a world and "invites us to a higher degree of critical consciousness about the invisible milieu in which we worship."[32]

Her appropriation of Schüssler Fiorenza draws heavily on a hermeneutics of suspicion as a primary interpretive posture, not only asking hard questions of texts but also of sermons themselves. Rhetorical critical analysis explores persuasive speech or texts to discover what values, actions, and commitments are being sponsored by the writer/speaker. Any rhetorical act, whether written or spoken, is subject to such an analysis. The rhetorical critic attends to those claims that are made explicit, the claims that are implied, and the claims that are rendered invisible or problematic in some way. Rhetorical critical analysis considers the choice of rhetorical strategies (structure of the argument) and what authorities are cited to lend credibility; the choice of language (how the words are put together, gathering their meaning through intimate relationship to other words); and the choices of metaphors, images, and illustrations.

Schüssler Fiorenza's approach to rhetorical products (particularly to texts) gives special attention to the "loadedness" of language and its power to influence ways of thinking. Schüssler Fiorenza claims that all rhetorical acts inscribe power and powerlessness and consequently can be used for or against liberation. "Rhetorical analysis seeks not only to disclose the means with which authors or interpreters attempt to persuade or motivate their audience, but also to trace the power-relations inscribed in the text and their functions in a particular rhetorical situation and sociohistorical location."[33]

With particular regard to the African American preaching tradition, Cannon draws on the work of Isaac R. Clark. Dr. Clark, her homiletics

---

[31]Cannon, *Katie's Canon,* 118–19.
[32]Ibid., 116.
[33]Elisabeth Schüssler Fiorenza, *Revelation: Vision of a Just World* (Minneapolis: Fortress Press, 1991), 21.

professor at ITC, had charged Cannon, just before his death, to carry on his homiletical legacy.[34] Clark defined preaching as *"divine activity wherein the Word of God is proclaimed or announced concerning contemporary issues with a view toward ultimate response to God."* Cannon's discussion of each element of the definition is instructive. *Divine activity* refers to the mediating relationship the preacher assumes between God and the congregation. Cannon insists that the preacher himself or herself is not the locus of authority, but that God's authority stands beyond the preacher as a guiding force, for the benefit of the hearers. Without teasing out the full implications of this definition, Cannon deftly undercuts questions about who has the authority to preach. Authority for preaching is not related to the preacher, but to God. In a separate interview, Cannon reflects on the question of women preachers: "I thought of all those brothers who told me their sins all the time—yet they got up and preached every Sunday. I remembered the biblical characters with clay feet. God doesn't call perfect people; God calls people who live in the world to tell the story. So I learned how to deliver sermons."[35]

In Cannon's view, The *Word of God* is a living word and is not necessarily confined to the biblical witness. The word becomes flesh and dwells among us as words from the Bible, as words from the preacher, as the presence of Jesus Christ's work, person, and ministry. "The God-self is present as the content of the preached word."[36] She insists that God is present as "the kerygmatic Christ" who pulsates with a "particular contemporaneity" that emphasizes the "close union of heaven and earth, God and people."[37] Cannon doesn't develop a homiletical christology, but certainly hints that her approach to the scripture, while traditionally respectful, is not ultimately grounded on scripture's own status, but on the kind of God who becomes present in preaching. "In the final analysis it is not the historical Jesus who occupies the central place, but the divine power that holds sway over him as the Word Incarnate."[38]

Proclamation or announcement is concerned with the orality/aurality of the event of preaching. Cannon, like Mitchell, urges preachers to use ordinary language—particularly the language of the community, including

[34]Risher, "Giving Forward," 28.
[35]Ibid.
[36]Cannon, *Katie's Canon,* 117.
[37]Ibid.
[38]Ibid.

idiom and colloquialism—and to assume a call-and-response interaction with the congregation. Cannon attaches theological meanings of resurrection to this dynamic mode of presentation; the preacher's use of language and the congregational response form an expression of new life, resurrection. She urges preachers to use whatever strategies will make the sermon "come alive," whether stories, anthropomorphisms, or folk wisdom.[39]

Contemporary issues refers to the necessity to make the sermon as fully contextualized to the congregation as possible, speaking to "historical and social events in the African American community, engaging knowledge in the arena where human beings struggle with one another."[40] Cannon's discussion of the contemporaneity of preaching suggests that the text take its clues less from ancient sociohistorical realities embedded in exegetical issues and more from the existential realities of the African American lifeworld, "sloughing off memories that no longer have relevance while proclaiming the religious inheritance of ancestral mothers and fathers that enhances narrative variation for audience response in new situations."[41] Cannon seems to be arguing that the authoritative interpretive community is the African American faith community, not some other group or scholarly body outside it. If this is indeed what she is arguing, it's a significant claim, closer to Henry Mitchell's claims about the oral tradition not only of the Bible, but of the African American faith community. Such a claim would fall short of the kind of radical biblical authority promoted by Massey.

The purpose of preaching, according to Cannon's understanding of Clark, is to promote and enable an *ultimate response* to God. Neither Clark nor Cannon would deny the emotional dimension of this response, but neither would they require emotional response to precede other types of responses. Where Henry Mitchell recognizes a number of behavioral *purposes* for any particular sermon, Cannon recognizes a number of legitimate *responses.* "According to Clark, the Black preacher's primary activity is to inform, engage, and point out the contradictions within situations of complacent security in order to invite the congregation to make a decision for or against emancipatory praxis."[42] Cannon, an ethicist, articulates a homiletic purpose similar to Samuel Proctor's, arguing that contradictions must be surfaced so that the faith community

---

[39]Ibid.
[40]Ibid., 118.
[41]Ibid.
[42]Ibid.

recognizes what Proctor might term the "antithetical." Where Henry Mitchell urges us to focus on celebration "in spite of," Cannon claims that "the constant exposure to the abounding iniquity of the world opens the congregation to a gracious message of deliverance."[43] Her understanding of the faith community seems to be closer to James Forbes's assumptions about an activist ecclesiology, where the church commits, as a whole body, to particular forms of emancipatory practice, or liberation practices.

Here is where Cannon engages her hermeneutics of suspicion, moving beyond issues of race and into issues of gender and class. Without diminishing the prophetic tradition within African American preaching, she concludes that race is not the only prophetic issue for the black church. "In appreciating the complexity of the genius of Black preaching, we must be able to analyze how this genre is both sacred and profane, active and passive, life-giving and death-dealing."[44] She charges the male-dominated pulpit with promoting images and interpretations of African American women that have undermined women's self-esteem and diminished their value to the community.

> Until recently Black preaching has not asked questions about womanist interpretation and womanist theological studies have not included homiletics...When sermons are written and presented in the interest of men, the categorical definitions of theoethical concepts lend an evidently weighty authority to androcentric conclusions about male preachers and masculine-centered culture. It is therefore important to analyze sermonic texts in terms of their socioecclesial locations and theological interests, with special attention to their gender dimension.[45]

For Cannon, following Schüssler Fiorenza, the "loadedness" of language, particularly preaching language, had functioned predominantly in the African American community in ways that reinforced the local power of African American males (particularly preachers) and that relegated women to second-class citizenship within their own faith communities. Cannon wants to use a rhetorical critical approach to explore womanist concerns of class, gender, and race to discover how sermons

---

[43]Ibid.
[44]Ibid., 120.
[45]Ibid., 113.

participate in creating or sustaining oppressive or liberating theoethical values and sociopolitical practices...how and when women are mentioned and whether these sermons adequately reflect African American reality ...challeng[ing] conventional biblical interpretations that characterize African American women as "sin-bringing Eve," "wilderness-whimpering Hagar," "hen-pecking Jezebel," "whoring Gomer," "prostituting Mary Magdalene," and "conspiring Sapphira"...The task of womanist homiletics is to unearth what Black preachers are saying about women.[46]

Cannon is concerned with not only issues of race and gender but also with issues of classism, claiming elsewhere that "much of what has been interpreted as race privilege or oppression is class injury."[47] Cannon is concerned with elitism in all forms, whether it surfaces in ideologies of race, gender, ageism, or heterosexism. Again, her concerns are in greater sympathy with James Forbes's own critiques, and should be likewise familiar to those who have studied Cone's later work.[48]

Cannon concludes her essay on preaching and womanist interpretation by raising three queries: how meaning is constructed, whose interests are served, and what kind of worlds are envisioned in black sacred rhetoric.[49] The shift toward imagination, language, and rhetoric is accompanied by a strong womanist critique of worldly power that creates an opening for a variety of homiletic convergences.

Teresa L. Fry Brown

Teresa L. Fry Brown is assistant professor of homiletics at Candler School of Theology, Emory University, Atlanta, Georgia. She attended Central Missouri State University (B.S., 1974; M.S., 1975), and received her Master of Divinity (1988) and Ph.D. (1996) at Iliff School of Theology. She is an ordained minister in the African Methodist Episcopal Church, and has published sermons and essays in *Those Preachin' Women, The Abingdon Women's Preaching Annual,* and *Preaching Justice.* Her first book, *God Don't Like Ugly: African American Women Handing on Spiritual*

---

[46]Ibid., 114.

[47]Risher, "Giving Forward," 28.

[48]See Rufus Burrow, Jr., *James H. Cone and Black Liberation Theology* (Jefferson, N.C.: McFarland & Co., 1994). Burrow explores the trajectory of certain themes and interests in Cone's work through three intellectual shifts.

[49]Cannon, *Katie's Canon,* 121.

Values, was published in 2000. She is active in the Academy of Homiletics and the American Academy of Religion, and her research interests include homiletics with an emphasis in African American and womanist styles, and womanist ethics, sociology, and history focusing on African American spiritual values.

She was born in 1951 and grew up as a "Black Baptist in Missouri."[50] Fry Brown begins her essay "Renovating Sorrow's Kitchen" with the observation that she has heard at least three thousand sermons, "90 percent of which were preached by Black men."[51] Her reference to "sorrow's kitchen" comes from Zora Neale Hurston's autobiographical comment, "I've been in sorrow's kitchen and licked out all the pots. Then I have been on peaky mountains wrapped in rainbows with a harp and a sword in my hands."[52] Fry Brown's use of this phrase for her essay title is an indication of the ambivalence she has experienced as a woman in the African American church. Her essay on preaching moves back and forth between these two poles: sorrow and peaky moments.

She recalls hearing her first woman evangelist when she was eighteen years old, "fascinated, frightened, and frustrated" as the woman preached from the floor at a musical. Fry Brown's reaction was due to the fact that she was sure the woman was going to hell, "since women just did not do that kind of thing."[53] Her comment is surely reminiscent of Ella Mitchell's experience of preaching from the floor. Since Fry Brown has become an ordained minister, a preacher, and a teacher of preachers, it's safe to assume that she has reconsidered her initial evaluation of the woman's spiritual destiny.

Her frustration has continued, however, as she has continued to write and speak about the unappreciated and devalued gifts of African American women to the church. Even if African American women have been silenced in the pulpit, they have nevertheless spoken clearly in families, communities, and churches. Fry Brown's *God Don't Like Ugly* explores the moral influence of mothers, grandmothers, sisters, play cousins, and othermothers, particularly through the oral tradition. Fry Brown's book considers the way extended family systems operate within African American life to impart spiritual values and Christian

---

[50]Fry Brown, "Renovating Sorrow's Kitchen," 43.
[51]Ibid.
[52]Zora Neale Hurston, *Dust Tracks on a Road* (New York: Harper Perennial, 1991), 205.
[53]Fry Brown, "Renovating Sorrow's Kitchen," 43.

identity to children. She surveys music, prayer, literature, folk tales, and sayings.

The impetus for her project is the phenomenon of negative stereotyping of African American women, not only from the African American pulpit, but primarily from white culture. Fry Brown cites the 1965 Moynihan Report "The Negro Family: The Case For National Action," which singled out single-parent African American homes and characterized them as dysfunctional when compared with white households. In addition, the Moynihan Report seemed to focus much of the blame on African American women as "castrating matriarchs," suggesting they were responsible for the alleged disintegration of the African American family.[54]

Fry Brown's goal in *God Don't Like Ugly* is to provide a more holistic picture of African American women, particularly as they participate in faith communities and families as wisdom-bearers and spiritual mothers. Fry Brown acknowledges that African American men may dominate the pulpit, but claims they by no means dominate the spiritual direction of communities. "There has been an unwritten assumption in our society that black men, following a patriarchal model, are the leaders of the black family, church, and community with an often intentional denial of the importance or presence of women as viable teachers, leaders, or nurturers of their children...The voice of African American women has been muted."[55]

For our current purposes, one of the most interesting aspects of Fry Brown's book for homiletics is that she reconstructs an alternative community of oral discourse, consisting of the moral wisdom of folk sayings, prayers, and songs of African American women. She surveys more than this, of course, including literature and autobiographical works by African American women, but even her survey of literature highlights the nature of this alternative community of oral discourse. Bluntly, in the African American community, not everybody talking about God is a preacher or a man.

Mother Wit, Wisdom Bearers, Sistuh Girlfriends, and othermothers all contribute to function in concert with the primary objectives of the church, to offer survival strategies, models of dignity, interpretations

---

[54]Teresa L. Fry Brown, *God Don't Like Ugly: African American Women Handing on Spiritual Values* (Nashville: Abingdon Press, 2000), 31–33. Fry Brown cites pages 5 and 35 of the Moynihan Report, which was based on census data collected between 1940 and 1963.

[55]Ibid., 15.

of salvation and conversion, knowledge of the Bible, praises of God, trust in Jesus, commitments to justice, and modes of ethical behavior. Those who are familiar with Katie Cannon's work will see the influence, sometimes implicit and sometimes explicit, in Fry Brown's work. Cannon's earliest book drew on the writing of Zora Neale Hurston to argue that African American women had and continue to have their own sources of theological reflection and moral formation: in the stories and lives of women themselves.[56]

Fry Brown's essay on womanist interpretation and preaching is consistent with her claims about women's spirituality. She agrees with Cannon's critique of images used by many African American male preachers, and offers alternative images, drawing not only on African *American* religious life and tradition but on African traditions as well.

> The ecclesiastical apartheid evident in twentieth-century churches is part of the assimilation of dominant cultural values that numerous Black denominations have undergone over the past two hundred years. A sort of cultural amnesia has been demonstrated by the men who stood with women for freedom of the race...In Africa women were essential to the cultural and religious practices of the community. North American slave narratives spoke of women priests, prophetesses, and queen mothers. Female griots, or storytellers, were the memory banks for the large genealogies of African Americans. Women were the prayer warriors who participated in all forms of worship.[57]

Fry Brown insists that African American women, lay and clergy, find their own experiences in the Bible, and offer alternative theological interpretations of traditional stories and images. She draws on the work of Renita Weems, womanist Hebrew Bible scholar at Vanderbilt Divinity School, to urge women to become hermeneuts themselves. "Interpretation depends on social location of the preacher and her particular hermeneutic, imagination, and creativity. Marginalized readers have the task and responsibility of restoring oppressed voices,

---

[56]I'm referring to Cannon's *Black Womanist Ethics* (Atlanta: Scholars Press, 1988), where she develops the categories of invisible dignity, quiet grace, and unshouted courage.

[57]Fry Brown, "Renovating Sorrow's Kitchen," 49. See also my work on African women theologians who make similar claims about the contemporary African context after Christianization, in L. Susan Bond, *Trouble with Jesus: Women, Christology, and Preaching* (St. Louis: Chalice Press, 1999), 101–7.

breaking the chains from the texts, and opening them up to all persons."[58] Fry Brown sees this alternative hermeneutical consciousness as something that lay and clergy women engage as colleagues. She also draws on the work of Jacquelyn Grant, Melva Wilson Costen, and Cheryl Townsend Gilkes. In terms of her sources and dialogue partners, Fry Brown leans more toward an Afrocentric approach.

Other Voices

What follows is a brief discussion of other African American women involved in theological education whose work contributes to emerging black feminist and womanist developments in homiletic theory. Many are well-published in other areas, but also have made implicit contributions to homiletic theory or reflections on preaching.

Melva Wilson Costen is the Helmar Emil Nielsen Professor of Worship and Music, chairperson of the Worship and Music Department, director of the African American Worship Traditions Program, and choral music director at the Interdenominational Theological Center in Atlanta, Georgia. Dr. Costen served as chair of the committee to develop the *Presbyterian Hymnal: Hymns, Psalms and Spiritual Songs* (Louisville: Westminster/John Knox Press, 1990). She also served on the committee that developed the "Directory of Worship" published in the *Presbyterian Book of Common Worship* (Louisville: Westminster/John Knox Press, 1993). She received her Ph.D. from Georgia State University in 1978.

Wilson Costen synthesizes a wealth of material in her look at the worship legacy of the African American Christian tradition. She assumes that worship is more than liturgical documents, especially "if those documents exclude the history and culture of those whose understanding of God in Jesus the Christ is uniquely contextualized in suffering and struggle."[59] Costen approaches the task by claiming three constants. First is the ethos of praise and celebration empowered by freedom in Christ. This attention to celebration puts her in agreement with Henry Mitchell, even if it's not as clear whether Wilson Costen is arguing for emotional or ritual understandings of celebration.[60]

---

[58]Fry Brown, "Renovating Sorrow's Kitchen," 54. Readers interested in Weems's work should begin with *Just a Sister Away: A Womanist Vision of Women's Relationships in the Bible* (San Diego: LuraMedia Press, 1988); *I Asked for Intimacy: Stories of Blessings, Birthings, and Betrayals* (San Diego: LuraMedia Press, 1993); and *Battered Love: Marriage, Sex, and Violence in the Hebrew Prophets,* Overtures to Biblical Theology (Philadelphia: Fortress Press, 1995).

[59]Melva Wilson Costen, *African American Christian Worship* (Nashville: Abingdon Press, 1993), 9.

[60]Ibid., 104–6.

The second constant is the inheritance of a shared African primal worldview that collapses secular and sacred into a more holistic understanding of experience. Inclusion of African retentions places Costen intellectually in the Herskovits tradition, though her synthetic approach is less concerned with form and function. Her philosophical nuance (informed by African philosopher John S. Mbiti) appropriates African retentions with regard to theological meaning, overcoming simplistic reductions to ritual form.

The third is the context of slavery. Through an Afro-Christian-liberation hermeneutic she traces slave worship in the Invisible Institution: the secret gatherings in "brush arbors"; the African model of the griot/priest for slave preachers; the priority of music, dance, and prayer; the sacramental attitude toward physical activity; and call and response. In "Praise House Worship," Costen examines the institutionalizing of slave worship into public form and the antecedents for the African American church as an all-encompassing social entity. She sets this discussion within the context of the spirituals, black hymnody, antebellum revivalism, and the continued synthesis of African and American frontier church elements.

Wilson Costen doesn't devote much attention to preaching and certainly does not discuss homiletic theory or method. She lists preaching as one of the four pillars of African American Christian worship, in addition to prayer, song, and testimony. Her work is primarily written within the intersection of African American history and liturgical theory and doesn't treat preaching except as it participates in liturgical activity.

Wilson Costen offers some hopeful direction by characterizing narrative preaching as the use of language, symbols, and symbolic actions, but does not discuss how language and symbol might be liberating. Her work is promising since it picks up on some of the themes of ritual theory and language theory that could be in conversation not only with the African American *male* homileticians but also with Katie Cannon's work. Her work also provides common ground for current homiletic theory (and hermeneutics) offered by white feminists.

Cheryl Townsend Gilkes is the John D. and Catherine T. MacArthur Associate Professor of Sociology and African American Studies and the director of the African American Studies Program at Colby College in Waterville, Maine. She is an ordained minister of the Union Baptist Church in Cambridge, Massachusetts, and author of *"If It Wasn't for the Women...": Black Women's Experience and Womanist Culture in Church and*

Community. Gilkes is particularly interested in a sociology of African American women, exploring their actual contributions to African American religious and cultural life, as well as to American public life in general. Her book title states her major thesis, that African American life, and particularly the Afro-Christian tradition, are (and historically *have* been) more radically dependent on African American women than popular assumptions or stereotypes would indicate. Her work supports on a sociohistorical level what Teresa Fry Brown claims at the level of domestic and familial relationships: African American women are powerful moral and ethical resources for transmitting values and teaching justice.

> If it wasn't for the women, racially oppressed communities would not have the institutions, organizations, strategies, and ethics that enable the group not only to survive or to maintain itself as an integral whole, but also to develop in an alien, hostile, oppressive situation and to challenge it. In spite of their powerlessness, African-American women and women of color generally have a dramatic impact within and beyond their communities.[61]

Gilkes has also written extensively about African American women in the "sanctified church," which is a general term "including the Holiness movement of the late nineteenth and early twentieth centuries and with the Pentecostal movement of the early twentieth century."[62] She has explored the role of women in the sanctified church in comparison with the roles of women in Baptist and Methodist communities of faith.

She has also explored the ways that women assume public leadership roles in communities of faith, including teaching and preaching responsibilities. Her discussion of biblical language, particularly as it constructs power and gender assumptions, is most relevant to discussions of homiletic theory. She acknowledges the problems that Katie Cannon cites, that preaching language and rhetoric have functioned in powerful ways to diminish African American women, but she claims that African American women have still been able to "find" themselves in sermons

---

[61]Cheryl Townsend Gilkes, *"If It Wasn't for the Women…": Black Women's Experience and Womanist Culture in Church and Community* (Maryknoll, N.Y.: Orbis Books, 2001), 26–27.
[62]Ibid., 77.

in empowering and meaningful ways.[63] Her chapter "'Some Mother's Son and Some Father's Daughter': Issues of Gender, Biblical Language, and Worship," in *"If It Wasn't for the Women,"* explores the alternative discourse in sermons by African American males to claim that "women are not outsiders to its social production."[64]

Cheryl J. Sanders is associate professor of Christian ethics at Howard University School of Divinity. She also serves as senior pastor of the Third Street Church of God in Washington, D.C. Her books include *Living the Intersection: Womanism and Afrocentrism in Theology* (1995); *Empowerment Ethics for a Liberated People: A Path to African American Social Transformation* (1995); *Saints in Exile: The Holiness-Pentecostal Experience in African American Religion and Culture* (1996); and *Ministry at the Margins: The Prophetic Mission of Women, Youth & the Poor* (1997).

Sanders began her scholarship with her Harvard dissertation work on slave narratives and conversion experiences, where she argued for an African or Afrocentric hermeneutic for understanding the narratives. Her Afrocentric views have endured throughout her scholarship, along with what may be characterized as a theologically conservative approach to a Christian ethics.

Sanders's essay "The Woman as Preacher" explored homiletic content as it relates to gender. Sanders was interested in pursuing the differences between women's and men's preaching. She selected eighteen sermons by women and eighteen sermons by men and analyzed them according to five categories.[65] Following James Massey's definitions of *sermon forms,* she explored four basic sermon forms: expository, narrative, textual, or topical.[66] She found that men and women tended to favor topical or thematic preaching slightly, and that men used expository forms more often than women did. Sanders distinguishes

---

[63]This is similar to Renita Weems's work with laywomen and their identification with particular biblical women. For example, see Weems, *Just a Sister Away; I Asked for Intimacy;* and *Showing Mary: How Women Can Share Prayers, Wisdom, and the Blessings of God* (New York: Warner Books, 2002).

[64]Gilkes, *If It Wasn't for the Women,* 141.Gilkes doesn't limit this discussion to preaching, but includes prayer, testimony, and music to provide a holistic picture of the way women figure in the worship event.

[65]Cheryl J. Sanders, "The Woman as Preacher," in *African American Religious Studies: An Interdisciplinary Anthology,* ed. Gayraud Wilmore (Durham, N.C.: Duke University Press, 1989), 372–91. The sermons were drawn from three sermon anthologies: Robert T. Newbold, Jr., ed., *Black Preaching: Selected Sermons in the Presbyterian Tradition* (Philadelphia: Geneva Press, 1977); J. Alfred Smith, *Outstanding Black Sermons* (Valley Forge, Pa.: Judson Press, 1976); and Ella P. Mitchell, ed., *Those Preachin' Women.*

[66]From James Earl Massey, *Designing the Sermon: Order and Movement in Preaching* (Nashville: Abingdon Press, 1980), 21.

expository preaching from textual preaching primarily by the length of the text, claiming that expository sermons are based on longer textual selections.[67]

She surveyed the *use of biblical texts* relative to literary genres: narrative, prophecy, poetry, apocalyptic, or epistle. She also noted whether or not a text dealt specifically with women. Sanders discovered that gender did not produce any significant difference in the preference for either Hebrew Bible or New Testament texts, with men and women preaching roughly 40 percent of their sermons from Hebrew Bible texts and about 60 percent from New Testament texts. She discovered more difference in terms of genre preference, with women preaching less on narrative passages than the men (44 percent of women to 61 percent of the men), and more on epistles than the men (33 percent of the women and only 11 percent of the men). Surprisingly, the women did *not* show a preference for preaching from texts that made specific reference to women.[68]

Sanders's third category was *central themes.* The three most popular themes were the church and its mission (25 percent of the sermons), Christian virtues (19 percent), and racial identity (17 percent). The only themes peculiar to women preachers involved survival, healing, and ministry; men alone preached on the nature of God and/or Christ.[69]

The fourth category was the *use of inclusive language* with reference to God and persons. Of the women 89 percent used inclusive language to refer to persons, while only 44 percent of the men did so, and 61 percent of the women used other-than-masculine God-talk compared with 39 percent of the men.[70]

The fifth category was something she designated *homiletical tasks,* some of which might be similar to Henry Mitchell's "behavioral purposes." Sanders identified seventeen homiletical tasks: affirmation, celebration, ecclesiastical critique, social critique, exhortation, interpreting scripture, urging Christian commitment, observing a liturgical event, proclaiming a vision, quoting hymn lyrics, quoting lyrics from spirituals, quoting poetry, using drama, storytelling, teaching, testifying, and translating scripture into vernacular. She discovered that the most

---

[67]Sanders, "The Woman as Preacher," 373–74.

[68]Ibid., 375.

[69]Ibid., 375–76. Sanders doesn't describe how the category of "ministry" as a theme differs from the category of "the church and its mission." It might be the case that the women preached more about ordination or calls to ministry, reinforcing the women's increased interest in "testifying" as a homiletical task.

[70]Ibid., 376.

common homiletical task by far was the interpretation of scripture, but that there were noticeable differences on the other homiletical tasks. She concluded that women preachers attempted a greater average number of tasks in any one sermon (used more variety), and that women did more storytelling and testifying while men did more social critique.[71]

The significance of Sanders's work on women preachers, even though it predates the emerging body of womanist scholarship, is that it calls into question earlier claims made by male homileticians about theological themes that characterize African American preaching. What may be more accurate is to acknowledge that the work of earlier male African American homileticians is adequate to the task of making generalizations about black male preachers, but does not necessarily reflect the presence of particular topics or themes preferred by African American female preachers. Of particular interest are the issues of social critique and the nature of God, which seem to be slightly more masculine interests than feminine interests.

All in all, the women who are currently contributing to African American theology and religious thought will bring new dimensions to African American homiletic theory and homiletic method. Delores Williams's work in ethics, Jacquelyn Grant's work in theology, and Renita Weems's work in Hebrew Bible, along with the efforts of other African American feminists and womanists, will begin to show even more influence on the current generation of women as well as on the African American male scholars beginning to break into the homiletic world.

If we wanted to follow any particular issues, one of the most critical would be to note the additional hermeneutic of suspicion that the women bring to the study of biblical texts. If the African American preaching tradition was indeed founded on a suspicion of white preaching and white interpretive approaches, women's insights continue that trajectory into new territory. Certainly matters of gender and the social construction of women through sermons will be of interest, but even beyond gender issues is the class critique implied by a number of womanist scholars. Class critiques will carry many African American women scholars into collaborative work with other women of color and with women in developing nations, providing a different kind of ecumenical conversation (perhaps interfaith conversations) than has previously occurred. Katie Cannon's work, devoted to exploring

---

[71]Ibid., 376–88.

multiple structures of oppression, may provide homiletical models for a method of ordinary theological reflection within communities of believers.

Another figural issue is the sustained attention to language and how it forms communities, provides reinforcement for perspectives, projects a worldview, and unmasks privilege. Katie Cannon's attention to metaphor and orality puts her at the cutting edge of current homiletical theory. Gilkes's attention to female imagery and Sanders's attention to women's homiletic ways of sponsoring and illustrating theological ideas are likewise issues that are emerging within the homiletical guild. Teresa Fry Brown's attention to the moral wisdom of ordinary African American Christian women taps into an alternative and powerful community of oral discourse that will fund homiletical studies. Wilson Costen's attention to ritual behavior reinforces current scholarship within liturgical and ritual studies and could lead to fascinating overlaps with Evans Crawford's work and with Henry Mitchell's claims about celebration.

Even though it is beyond the limits of this project to explore possibilities suggested by the entire community of African American women theologians, it is clear that the emerging womanist scholarship will have a significant impact on homiletic thought, not just in the world of African American homiletic theory, but in the broadest arena of homiletic scholarship. We might expect to see ongoing homiletical appropriations of the two trajectories identified here as the dialogical womanists and the Afrocentric womanists. We will almost surely see increased attention to worldwide theological questions of marginalized populations, global poverty, issues of ecumenicity, and a sisterhood of color. The savvy homiletician or preacher will attend to the emerging contours to discover ways that interpretation, rhetoric, poetics, theology, and practices are informed by these women who see and hear and know what others do not. I particularly urge white homileticians to pay attention to womanist scholarship to see what such new perspectives might offer to homiletic theory and preaching the good news of God's amazing grace.

Further Reading

(Selections for chapter 1 compiled by Robert R. Howard. Material that relates specifically to preachers profiled in later chapters will be included in the lists for those chapters in chronological order.)

Chapter 1: African American Preaching and Homiletic Theory

Books

Beale, Lawrence L. *Toward a Black Homiletic.* New York: Vantage Press, 1978.

Blount, Brian K. *Go Preach!: Mark's Kingdom Message and the Black Church Today.* Maryknoll, N.Y.: Orbis Books, 1998.

Coleman, Will. *Tribal Talk: Black Theology, Hermeneutics, and African-American Ways of "Telling the Story."* University Park: Pennsylvania State University Press, 2000.

Crawford, Evans, with Thomas H. Troeger. *The Hum: Call and Response in African American Preaching.* Nashville: Abingdon Press, 1995.

Davis, Gerald R. *I Got the Word in Me and I Can Sing It, You Know: A Study of the Performed African-American Sermon.* Philadelphia: University of Philadelphia Press, 1985.

Felder, Cain Hope. *Troubling Biblical Waters: Race, Class, and Family.* Maryknoll, N.Y.: Orbis Books, 1989.

_____, ed. *Stony the Road We Trod: African American Biblical Interpretation.* Minneapolis: Fortress Press, 1991.

Hamilton, Charles V. *The Black Preacher in America.* New York: Morrow, 1972.

Harris, James. *Preaching Liberation.* Minneapolis: Fortress Press, 1995.

Hicks, H. Beecher, Jr. *Images of the Black Preacher.* Valley Forge, Pa.: Judson Press, 1977.

Hubbard, Dolan. *The Sermon and the African American Literary Imagination.* Columbia: University of Missouri Press, 1994.

Johnson, Joseph Andrew, Jr. *The Soul of the Black Preacher.* Philadelphia: Pilgrim Press, 1971.

Johnson-Smith, Robert, ed. *Wisdom of the Ages: The Mystique of the African American Preacher.* Valley Forge, Pa.: Judson Press, 1995.

Jones, Amos, Jr. *As You Go Preach!: Dynamics of Sermon Building and Preaching in the Black Church.* Nashville: Bethlehem Book, 1996.

LaRue, Cleophus J. *The Heart of Black Preaching.* Louisville: Westminster John Knox Press, 2000.

Lischer, Richard. *The Preacher King: Martin Luther King, Jr. and the Word That Moved America.* New York: Oxford University Press, 1995.

McClain, William B. *Come Sunday: The Liturgy of Zion.* Nashville: Abingdon Press, 1990.

McMickle, Marvin A. *Preaching to the Black Middle Class: Words of Challenge, Words of Hope.* Valley Forge, Pa.: Judson Press, 2000.

Miller, Keith D. *Voice of Deliverance: The Language of Martin Luther King, Jr., and Its Sources.* New York: Free Press, 1992.

Moyd, Olin P. *Preaching and Practical Theology: An African American Perspective.* Nashville: Townsend Press, 1994.

_____. *The Sacred Art: Preaching and Theology in the African American Tradition.* Valley Forge, Pa.:
    Judson Press, 1995.
Myers, William H. *The Irresistible Urge to Preach: A Collection of African American "Call" Stories.*
    Atlanta: Aaron Press, 1992.
Pipes, William H. *Say Amen, Brother! Old-Time Negro Preaching: A Study in American Frustration.*
    New York: William-Frederick Press, 1951.
Reid, Stephen Breck. *Experience and Tradition: A Primer in Black Biblical Hermeneutics.* Nashville:
    Abingdon Press, 1990.
Rosenberg, Bruce A. *The Art of the American Folk Preacher.* New York: Oxford University Press,
    1970.
Scott, Manuel. *From a Black Brother.* Nashville: Broadman Press, 1971.
Smith, J. Alfred, Sr. *For the Facing of This Hour: A Call to Action.* Elgin, Ill.: Progressive Baptist
    Publishing House, 1981.
_____. *New Treasures from the Old: A Guide to Preaching from the Old Testament.* Elgin, Ill.:
    Progressive National Baptist, 1987.
_____. *Preach On!* Nashville: Broadman Press, 1984.
Smith, Kelly Miller. *Social Crisis Preaching.* Macon, Ga.: Mercer University Press, 1984.
Stewart, Carlyle Fielding. *Joy Songs, Trumpet Blasts, and Hallelujah Shouts: Sermons in the African-
    American Preaching Tradition.* Lima, Ohio: CSS Publishing Co., 1997.
Stewart, Warren H. *Interpreting God's Word in Black Preaching.* Valley Forge, Pa.: Judson Press,
    1984.
Walker, Wyatt Tee. *The Soul of Black Worship.* New York: Martin Luther King Fellows Press,
    1984.
Warren, Mervyn. *Black Preaching: Truth and Soul.* Washington, D.C.: University Press of
    America, 1977.
Wimbush, Vincent L. *African Americans and the Bible: Sacred Texts and Social Textures.* New York:
    Continuum, 2000.

Articles in Journals and Essays in Books

Alvarez, Alexandra. "Martin Luther King's 'I Have a Dream': The Speech Event as Metaphor."
    Journal of Black Studies 18(1987–88): 337–57.
Atwater, Deborah F. "A Dilemma of Black Communication Scholars: The Challenge of
    Finding New Rhetorical Tools." *Journal of Black Studies* 15(1984): 5–16.
Baldwin, Lewis V. "The Minister as Preacher, Pastor, and Prophet: The Thinking of Martin
    Luther King, Jr." *American Baptist Quarterly* 7(June 1988): 79–97.
Blount, Marcellus. "The Preacherly Text: African American Poetry and Vernacular
    Performance." *Proceedings of the Modern Language Association* 107(1992): 582–93.
Condit, Celeste Michelle, and John Louis Lucaites. "Malcom X and the Rhetoric of
    Revolutionary Dissent." *Journal of Black Studies* 23(1992–93): 291–313.
Daniel, Jack L., and Geneva Smitherman. "How I Got Over: Communication Dynamics in
    the Black Community." *Quarterly Journal of Speech* 62(February 1976): 26–39.
Dionisopoulos, George A., and Victoria J. Gallagher, Steven R. Goldzwig, and David Zarefsky.
    "Martin Luther King, The American Dream, and Vietnam: A Collision of Rhetorical
    Trajectories." *Western Journal of Communications* 56(1992): 91–107.
Earl, Riggins R. "The Black Church, Black Women, and the Call." *Liturgy* 7/4(Spring 1989):
    87ff.
Franklin, Robert M. "The Safest Place on Earth: The Culture of Black Congregations." In
    New Perspectives in the Study of Congregations, vol. 2 of *American Congregations,* edited by
    James P. Wind and James W. Lewis. Chicago: University of Chicago Press, 1994,
    257–94, esp. 264–75.
Harris, James H. "Preaching Liberation: The Afro-American Sermon and the Quest for
    Social Change." *Journal of Religious Thought* 46/2(1989–90): 72–89.
Hayden, J. Carleton. "Black Episcopal Preaching in the Nineteenth Century: Intellect and
    Will." *Journal of Religious Thought* 39 (Spring/Summer 1982): 12–20.
Holt, Grace. "Stylin' Outta the Black Pulpit." In *Rappin' and Stylin' Out: Communication in Urban
    Black America,* edited by Thomas Kochman. Urbana: University of Illinois Press, 1972,
    189–204.

Hubbard, Dolan. "The Black Preacher Tale as Cultural Biography." *CLA (College Language Association) Journal* 30(1987): 328–42.

_____. "Toward a Definition of the African American Sermon." In *The Sermon and the African American Literary Imagination.* Columbia: University of Missouri Press, 1994, 1–25.

Illo, John. "The Rhetoric of Malcom X." *Columbia University Forum* 9/2(Spring 1966): 5–12.

McCarthy, S. Margaret. "The Afro-American Sermon and the Blues: Some Parallels." *The Black Perspective in Music* 4 (1976): 269–77.

Miller, Keith D. "Composing Martin Luther King, Jr." *Proceedings of the Modern Language Association* 105 (1990): 70–82.

_____. "Martin Luther King, Jr., and the Black Folk Pulpit." *Journal of American History* 78 (1991): 120–23.

_____. "Taking a Ride on the 'Old Ship of Zion': Self-Making in African-American Folk Religion." In *Ethos: New Essays in Rhetorical and Critical Theory,* edited by James S. Baumlin and Tita French Baumlin. Dallas: Southern Methodist University Press, 1994, 319–39.

Moyd, Olin P. "Elements in Black Preaching." *Journal of Religious Thought* 30/1 (Spring/Summer 1973): 52–62.

Murphy, Larry G. "African American Worship and the Interpretation of Scripture." *Ex Auditu* 8 (1992): 95–106.

Niles, Lyndrey A. "Rhetorical Characteristics of Traditional Black Preaching." *Journal of Black Studies* 15 (1984): 41–52.

Pipes, William H. "Oldtime Negro Preaching: An Interpretive Study." *Quarterly Journal of Speech* 31 (1945): 15–21.

Pitts, Walter. "West African Poetics in the Black Preaching Style." *American Speech* 64 (1989): 137–49.

Roberts, J. Deotis. "Black Religion." *Mid-Stream* 22 (1983): 378–85.

Smith, Arthur L. "Markings of an African Concept of Rhetoric." *Today's Speech* 19 (Spring 1971): 13–18.

_____. "Socio-Historical Perspectives of Black Oratory." *Quarterly Journal of Speech* 56 (1970): 264–69.

Stone, Sonja H. "Oral Tradition and Spiritual Drama: The Cultural Mosaic for Black Preaching." *Journal of the Interdenominational Theological Center* 8 (Fall 1980): 17–27.

Sermon Collections

Aldred, Joe, ed. *Preaching With Power: Sermons by Black Preachers.* New York: Cassell, 1998.

Benn, J. Solomon. *Preaching in Ebony.* Grand Rapids, Mich.: Baker Book House, 1981.

Hicks, H. Beecher, Jr. *Preaching through a Storm.* Grand Rapids, Mich.: Ministry Resources Library, 1987.

Lofton, Fred C., ed. *Our Help in Ages Past: Sermons from Morehouse. (In Memory of Dr. Benjamin Elijah Mays, 1894–1984).* Elgin, Ill.: Progressive National Baptist, 1987.

Newbold, Robert T., Jr., ed. *Black Preaching: Select Sermons in the Presbyterian Tradition.* Philadelphia: Geneva Press, 1977.

Philpot, William M., ed. *Best Black Sermons.* Valley Forge, Pa.: Judson Press, 1972.

Ponder, Rhinold, and Michelle Tuck-Ponder, eds. *The Wisdom of the Word: Love: Great African-American Sermons.* New York: Crown Publishers, 1997.

Ray, Sandy F. *Journeying through a Jungle.* Nashville: Broadman Press, 1979.

Reid, Frank Madison, III, Jeremiah A. Wright, Jr., and Colleen Birchett. *When Black Men Stand Up for God: Reflections on the Million Man March.* Chicago: African American Images, 1996.

Ross, Jini Kilgore, ed. *What Makes You So Strong?: Sermons of Joy and Strength from Jeremiah A. Wright, Jr.* Valley Forge, Pa.: Judson Press, 1993.

Smith, J. Alfred, Sr., ed. *No Other Help I Know: Sermons on Prayer and Spirituality.* Valley Forge, Pa.: Judson Press, 1996.

_____, ed. *Outstanding Black Sermons.* Valley Forge, Pa.: Judson Press, 1976.

Stewart, Carlyle Fielding. *Joy Songs, Trumpet Blasts, and Hallelujah Shouts: Sermons in the African-American Preaching Tradition.* Lima, Ohio: CSS Publishing Co., 1997.

Thurman, Michael, ed. *Voices from the Dexter Pulpit.* Montgomery, Ala.: NewSouth Books, 2001.

Waters, Kenneth L., Sr. *Afrocentric Sermons: The Beauty of Blackness in the Bible.* Valley Forge, Pa.: Judson Press, 1993.

Watley, William D. *Sermons on Special Days: Preaching through the Year in the Black Church.* Valley Forge, Pa.: Judson Press, 1987.

_____. *You Have to Face It to Fix It: Sermons on the Challenges of Life.* Valley Forge, Pa.: Judson Press, 1997.

_____, and Raquel Annette St. Clair. *The African Presence in the Bible: Gospel Sermons Rooted in History.* Valley Forge, Pa.: Judson Press, 2000.

Wright, Jeremiah A., Jr. *Good News!: Sermons of Hope for Today's Families.* Valley Forge, Pa.: Judson Press, 1995.

Young, Henry J., ed. *Preaching the Gospel.* Philadelphia: Fortress Press, 1976.

_____, ed. *Preaching of Suffering and a God of Love.* Philadelphia: Fortress Press, 1978.

Works on or by James Hal Cone

Burrow, Rufus, Jr. *James H. Cone and Black Liberation Theology.* Jefferson, N.C.: McFarland & Co., 1994.

Cone, James H. *Black Theology and Black Power.* New York: Seabury Press, 1969.

_____. *A Black Theology of Liberation.* Philadelphia: Lippincott, 1970.

_____. *For My People: Black Theology and the Black Church.* Maryknoll, N.Y.: Orbis Books, 1984.

_____. *God of the Oppressed.* New York: Seabury Press, 1975.

_____. *Martin & Malcolm & America: A Dream or a Nightmare.* Maryknoll, N.Y.: Orbis Books, 1991.

_____. *My Soul Looks Back.* Nashville: Abingdon Press, 1982.

_____. *Risks of Faith: The Emergence of a Black Theology of Liberation, 1968–1998.* Boston: Beacon Press, 1999.

_____. *Speaking the Truth: Ecumenism, Liberation, and Black Theology.* Grand Rapids, Mich.: W. B. Eerdmans, 1986.

_____. *The Spirituals and The Blues.* New York: Seabury Press, 1972.

_____, and Gayraud Wilmore, eds. *Black Theology: A Documentary History, 1966–1979.* Maryknoll, N.Y.: Orbis Books, 1979.

Hopkins, Dwight N., ed. *Black Faith and Public Talk: Critical Essays on James H. Cone's Black Theology and Black Power.* Maryknoll, N.Y.: Orbis Books, 1999.

Stewart, Carlyle Fielding. *God, Being, and Liberation: A Comparative Analysis of the Theologies and Ethics of James H. Cone and Howard Thurman.* Lanham, Md.: University Press of America, 1989.

Townes, Emilie M. "The Kingdom of God in Black Preaching: An Analysis and Critique of James H. Cone." D. Min. thesis, University of Chicago Divinity School, 1982.

Chapter 2: Samuel DeWitt Proctor

Books

Proctor, Samuel DeWitt. *The Young Negro in America, 1960–1980.* New York: Association Press, 1966.

_____. with William D. Watley. *Sermons from the Black Pulpit.* Valley Forge, Pa.: Judson Press, 1984.

_____. *Preaching about Crises in the Community.* Philadelphia: Westminster Press, 1988.

_____. *My Moral Odyssey.* Valley Forge, Pa.: Judson Press, 1989.

_____. *How Shall They Hear?: Effective Preaching for Vital Faith.* Valley Forge, Pa.: Judson Press, 1992.

_____. *The Certain Sound of the Trumpet: Crafting a Sermon of Authority.* Valley Forge, Pa.: Judson Press, 1994.

_____. *The Substance of Things Hoped For: A Memoir of African American Faith.* New York: G. P. Putnam's Sons, 1995.

_____, and Gardner C. Taylor with Gary V. Simpson. *We Have This Ministry: The Heart of the Pastor's Vocation.* Valley Forge, Pa.: Judson Press, 1996.

Selected Essays and Articles in Journals

____. "Prescription for Change: Improving the Future for Black Americans: A Symposium by Seven Black Religious Leaders." *Christian Century* 95 (January 18, 1978): 47–51.

____. "The Black Community and the New Religious Right." *Foundations* 25 (April-June 1982): 180–87.

____. "The Theological Validation of Black Worship" [reply by Jacquelyn Grant]. *Journal of the Interdenominational Theological Center* 14 (Fall 1986–Spring 1987): 211–23.

____. "The Black Church and the Crises in the Black Community." *Chicago Theological Seminary Register* 80 (Spring 1990): 5–10.

____. "The Metes and Bounds of Black Theology." *Journal of Theology* (United Theological Seminary) 96 (1992): 33–41.

Chapter 3: Gardner Calvin Taylor

Books

Taylor, Gardner C., *How Shall They Preach: The Lyman Beecher Lectures and Five Lenten Sermons.* Elgin, Ill.: Progressive Baptist Publishing House, 1977.

____. *The Scarlet Thread.* Elgin, Ill.: Progressive Baptist Publishing House, 1981.

____. *Chariots Aflame.* Nashville: Broadman Press, 1988.

Chapters in Books

____. "Some Comments on Race Hate." In *The Pulpit Speaks,* edited by Alfred T. Davies. New York: Harper & Row, 1965.

____. "Why I Believe There Is a God." In *Why I Believe There Is a God,* edited by Howard Thurman. Chicago: Johnson Publishing Co., 1965.

____. "Introduction." In *Best Black Sermons,* edited by William M. Philpot. Valley Forge, Pa.: Judson Press, 1972.

____. "Shaping Sermons by the Shape of Text and Preacher." In *Preaching Biblically,* edited by Don M. Wardlaw. Philadelphia: Westminster Press, 1983.

Articles in Journals

____. "Climbing Jacob's Ladder." *Harvard Divinity Bulletin* 22, no. 4 (1993): 9–10.

____. "Black Freedom Fighters." *Christian Century* 112 (August 16–23 1995): 777–78.

____. "God Is Still on the Throne." *Living Pulpit* 6, no. 1 (January-March 1997): 13.

Interviews with Taylor

Duduit, Michael. "Preaching and the Power of Words." *Preaching* 9 (January/February 1994): 2–8.

Strobel, Lee. "Timeless Tension: How Can Preachers Bring the Unchanging Scripture to a Changing World?" *Leadership* 16 (Fall 1995): 18–27.

Chapter 4: James Earl Massey

Books

Callen, Barry L., ed. *Sharing Heaven's Music: The Heart of Christian Preaching, Essays in Honor of James Earl Massey.* Nashville: Abingdon Press, 1995.

Massey, James Earl. *An Introduction to the Negro Churches in the Church of God Reformation Movement.* New York: Shining Light Press, 1957.

____. *When Thou Prayest: An Interpretation of Christian Prayer According to the Teachings of Jesus.* Anderson, Ind.: Warner Press, 1960.

____. *The Worshiping Church: A Guide to the Experience of Worship.* Anderson, Ind.: Warner Press, 1961.

____. *The Soul Under Siege: A Fresh Look at Christian Experience.* Anderson, Ind.: Warner Press, 1970.

____. *The Hidden Disciplines.* Anderson, Ind.: Warner Press, 1972.

____. *The Responsible Pulpit.* Anderson, Ind.: Warner Press, 1974.

____. *The Sermon in Perspective: A Study of Communication and Charisma.* Grand Rapids, Mich.: Baker Book House, 1976.

____. *Concerning Christian Unity: A Study of the Relational Imperative of Agape Love.* Anderson, Ind.: Warner Press, 1979.

____. *Designing the Sermon: Order and Movement in Preaching.* Nashville: Abingdon Press, 1980.

____, ed., with Wayne McCown. *Interpreting God's Word For Today: An Inquiry into Hermeneutics from a Biblical-Theological Perspective, Volume 2.* Anderson, Ind.: Warner Press, 1982.

____. *The Burdensome Joy of Preaching.* Nashville: Abingdon Press, 1998.

____. *Sundays in the Tuskegee Chapel: Selected Sermons.* Nashville: Abingdon Press, 2000.

Selected Chapters in Books

____. "Teaching Homiletics to Black Seminarians: Some Essential Methods," in *Papers for the Annual Meeting of the Academy of Homiletics, 1977.*

____. "The Preacher's Rhetoric." In *A Celebration of Ministry: Essays in Honor of Frank Bateman Stanger,* edited by Kenneth Cain Kinghorn. Wilmore, Ky.: Francis Asbury Publishing Co., 1982.

____. "Thurman's Preaching: Substance and Style." In *God and Human Freedom: A Festschrift in Honor of Howard Thurman,* edited by Henry J. Young. Richmond, Ind.: Friends United Press, 1983.

____. "On Being a Preacher." In *Educating for Service: Essays in Honor of Robert H. Reardon,* edited by James Earl Massey. Anderson, Ind.: Warner Press, 1984.

____. "An African-American Model." In *Hermeneutics for Preaching: Approaches to Contemporary Interpretations of Scripture,* edited by Raymond Bailey. Nashville: Broadman Press, 1992.

____. "Application in the Sermon." In *A Handbook of Contemporary Preaching,* edited by Michael Duduit. Nashville: Broadman Press, 1992.

____. "Reading the Bible as African Americans." In *The New Interpreters Bible.* Vol. 1. Nashville: Abingdon Press, 1994.

____. "Preaching Truth in an Age of Doubt." In *The Abingdon Preaching Annual 1995,* edited by Michael Duduit. Nashville: Abingdon Press, 1994.

____. "The Preacher Who Would Be a Teacher." In *Preaching on the Brink,* edited by Martha J. Simmons. Nashville: Abingdon Press, 1996.

Selected Articles in Journals

____. "On Being a Preacher," *Covenant Quarterly* (February 1988): 3–11.

____. "Planning for Worship at Tuskegee Chapel," *Review and Expositor* (Winter 1988): 71–78.

____. "The Dream of Community," *The Princeton Seminary Bulletin* 9, no. 3 (1988): 211–12.

____. "Hermeneutics for Preaching," *Review and Expositor* 90, no. 3 (Summer 1993): 359–69.

Chapter 5: James Alexander Forbes, Jr.

Books

Forbes, James A. Jr. *The Holy Spirit and Preaching.* Nashville: Abingdon Press, 1989.

Chapters in Books

____. "What Is Preaching?–A Response." In *A New Look At Preaching,* edited by John Burke, O. P. Wilmington, Del.: Michael Glazier, 1983.

____. "Preaching in the Contemporary World." In *For Creation's Sake: Preaching, Ecology, and Justice,* edited by Dieter T. Hessel. Philadelphia: Geneva Press, 1985.

____. "Whatever Happened to the Golden Rule?" In *Envisioning the New City: A Reader on Urban Ministry,* edited by Eleanor Scott Meyers. Louisville: Westminster/John Knox Press, 1992.

____. "Introduction: More Light from the Spirit on Sexuality." In *Homosexuality and Christian Faith: Questions of Conscience For the Churches,* edited by Walter Wink. Minneapolis: Fortress Press, 1999, 1–9.

Articles in Journals

____. "Ministry of Hope from a Double Minority," *Theological Education* 9 suppl (Summer 1973): 305–26.

____. "Resurrection and the Courage to Die." *Christianity and Crisis* 48 (March 21, 1988): 75–76.

____. "Preaching on the Eve of a New Millennium." Inaugural Address. *Union Seminary Quarterly Review* 42, no. 4 (1988): 17–23.

____. "Matters of the Heart." *Sojourners* 18, no. 5 (May 1989): 24–27.

____. "To Keep the Nation from Losing Its Soul." *Sojourners* 20 (August/September 1991): 24–25.

____. "New Wine: Telling the Truth of Our Need for Transformation." *Other Side* 31 (July/August 1996): 8–11.

____. "The Fate of African Americans." *Tikkun* 11 (September/October, 1996): 38–44.

Chapter 6: Henry Herbert Mitchell

Books

Mitchell, Henry H. *Black Preaching.* Philadelphia and New York: J. B. Lippincott, 1970. Reprint, New York: Harper & Row, 1979.

____. *Black Belief: Folk Beliefs of Blacks in America and West Africa.* New York: Harper & Row, 1975.

____. *The Recovery of Preaching.* San Francisco: Harper & Row, 1977.

____, and Nicholas Cooper-Lewter. *Soul Theology: The Heart of American Black Culture.* San Francisco: Harper & Row, 1986.

____. *Black Preaching: The Recovery of a Powerful Art.* Nashville: Abingdon Press, 1990.

____. *Celebration and Experience in Preaching.* Nashville: Abingdon Press, 1990.

____, and Martha J. Simmons. *A Study Guide to Accompany Celebration and Experience in Preaching.* Self-published. 1993.

____, and Emil M. Thomas. *Preaching For Black Self-Esteem.* Nashville: Abingdon Press, 1994.

____, and Ella Pearson Mitchell. *Together for Good: Lessons from Fifty-Five Years of Marriage.* Kansas City: Andrews McMeel Publishing, 1999.

Martha J. Simmons, ed. *Preaching on the Brink: The Future of Homiletics: In Honor of Henry H. Mitchell.* Nashville: Abingdon Press, 1996.

Chapters in Books

____. "The Justice of God." In *Biblical Preaching: An Expositor's Treasury,* edited by James W. Cox. Philadelphia: Westminster Press, 1983.

____. "Black Preaching." In *Black Church Life-Styles,* edited by Emmanuel L. McCall. Nashville: Broadman Press, 1986.

____. "Toward a Theology of Black Preaching." In *African American Religious Studies: An Interdisciplinary Anthology,* edited by Gayraud S. Wilmore. Durham, N.C.: Duke University Press, 1989.

____. "The Hearer's Experience of the Word." In *Listening to the Word: Studies in Honor of Fred B. Craddock,* edited by Gail R. O'Day and Thomas Long. Nashville: Abingdon Press, 1993.

Selected Articles in Journals

____. "Celebration of a Stolen Gospel." *Home Missions* 43, no. 4 (April 1972).

____. "Black Improvisation! Real and Imitation." *Freeing the Spirit* 2, no. 4 (1973).

____. "Black Preaching." *Review and Expositor: A Baptist Theological Journal* 70, no. 3 (Summer, 1973).

____. "Some Preliminary Reflections on Authority in Black Religion." *Journal of the Interdenominational Theological Center* 3, no. 1 (1975).

____. "A Brief on Black Worship: Culture and Theology." *American Baptist Quarterly* 5, no. 4 (December 1985).

____. "On Preaching to the Whole Person." *Pulpit Digest* 68 (January/February and March/April 1988).

Chapter 7: African American Women and Womanists

Books, Articles, and Essays about African American Women and Womanists

Andrews, William L. *Sisters of the Spirit: Three Black Women's Autobiographies of the Nineteenth Century.* Bloomington: Indiana University Press, 1986.

Baldwin, Lewis V. "Black Women and African Union Methodism, 1813–1983." *Methodist History* 21(1982–83): 225–37.

Cannon, Katie G. "Womanist Interpretation and Preaching in the Black Church." *Searching the Scriptures.* Vol. 1 of *A Feminist Introduction,* edited by Elisabeth Schüssler Fiorenza. New York: Crossroad, 1993, 326–37.

Earl, Riggins R. "The Black Church, Black Women, and the Call." *Liturgy* 7/4(Spring 1989): 87ff.

Gilkes, Cheryl Townsend. "'Some Mother's Son and Some Father's Daughter': Gender and Biblical Language in Afro-Christian Worship Tradition." In *Shaping New Vision: Gender and Values in American Culture,* edited by Clarissa Atkinson, Constance H. Buchanan, and Margaret R. Miles. Vol. 5 of Harvard Women's Studies in Religion. Ann Arbor, Mich.: U. M. I. Research Press, 1987, 73–99.

Goode, Gloria Davis. *Preachers of the Word and Singers of the Gospel: The Ministry of Women among Nineteenth Century African-Americans.* Philadelphia: University of Pennsylvania, 1990.

Humez, Jean McMahon. "'My Spirit Eye': Some Functions of Spiritual and Visionary Experience in the Lives of Five Black Women Preachers, 1810–1880." In *Women and the Structure of Society: Selected Research from the Fifth Berkshire Conference on the History of Women,* edited by Barbara Harris and JoAnn K. McNamara. Durham, N.C.: Duke University Press, 1984, 129–43.

____. "Visionary Experience and Power: The Career of Rebecca Cox Jackson." In *Black Apostles at Home and Abroad: Afro-Americans and the Christian Mission from the Revolution to Reconstruction,* edited by David W. Wills and Richard Newman. Boston: G. K. Hall & Co., 1982.

____, ed. *Gifts of Power: The Writings of Rebecca Jackson, Black Visionary, Shaker Eldress.* Amherst: University of Massachusetts Press, 1981, especially 311–27, "Documents: Female Preaching and the A.M.E. Church, 1820–1852."

Kelly, Leontine T. C. "Preaching in the Black Tradition." In *Women Ministers,* edited by Judith L. Weidman. San Francisco: Harper & Row, 1985, 67–76.

Lee, Jarena. "A Female Preacher among the African Methodists." In *Afro-American Religious History: A Documentary Witness,* edited by Milton C. Sernett. Durham, N.C.: Duke University Press, 1985, 160–79.

Lincoln, C. Eric, and Lawrence H. Mamiya. "The Pulpit and the Pew: The Black Church and Women." In *The Black Church in the African American Experience.* Durham, N.C.: Duke University Press, 1990, 274–308.

Mitchell, Ella Pearson, ed. *Women: To Preach or Not To Preach: 21 Outstanding Black Preachers Say Yes!.* Valley Forge, Pa.: Judson Press, 1991.

____, and Henry H. Mitchell. *Together for Good: Lessons from Fifty-Five Years of Marriage.* Kansas City: Andrews McMeel Publishing, 1999.

Overton, Betty J. "Black Women Preachers: A Literary Overview." *Southern Quarterly* 23(Spring 1985): 157–66.

Peck, Catherine L. "Your Daughters Shall Prophesy: Women in the Afro-American Preaching Tradition." In *Diversities of Gifts: Field Studies in Southern Religion,* edited by Ruel W. Tyson, Jr., James L. Peacock, and Daniel Watkins Patterson. Urbana: University of Illinois Press, 1988, 143–56.

Sanders, Cheryl J. "The Woman as Preacher." *Journal of Religious Thought* 43/1(Spring/Summer 1986): 6–23. Reprinted in *African American Religious Studies: An Interdisciplinary Anthology,* edited by Gayraud Wilmore. Durham, N.C.: Duke University Press, 1989, 372–91.

Smith, Amanda Berry. *An Autobiography; the Story of the Lord's Dealings with Mrs. Amanda Smith, the Colored Evangelist; Containing an Account of Her Life Work of Faith, and Her Travels in America, England, Ireland, Scotland, India, and Africa, as an Independent Missionary.* Chicago: The Christian Witness Co., 1921. Reprint, New York: Oxford University Press, 1988.

Travis, J. Ruth. "Preaching Styles of Female Pastors in the African Methodist Episcopal Church, Baltimore Maryland." D.Min. thesis, United Theological Seminary, Dayton, Ohio, 1992.

Williams, Delores S. "Visions, Inner Voices, Apparitions, and Defiance in Nineteenth-Century Black Women's Narratives." *Women's Studies Quarterly* 21(1993): 81–89.

Sermon Collections

Collier-Thomas, Bettye. *Daughters of Thunder: Black Women Preachers and their Sermons, 1850–1979.* San Francisco: Jossey-Bass, 1997.

Cook, Suzan D. Johnson, and William D. Watley. *Preaching in Two Voices: Sermons on the Women in Jesus' Life.* Valley Forge, Pa.: Judson Press, 1992.

King, Bernice A., ed. *Hard Questions, Heart Answers: Speeches and Sermons.* New York: Broadway Books, 1996.

Milhaven, Annie Lally, ed. *Sermons Seldom Heard: Women Proclaim Their Lives.* New York: Crossroad, 1991.

Mitchell, Ella Pearson, ed. *Those Preachin' Women: Sermons by Black Women Preachers.* 3 Vols. Valley Forge, Pa.: Judson Press.

Newbold, Robert T., Jr., ed. *Black Preaching: Select Sermons in the Presbyterian Tradition.* Philadelphia: Geneva Press, 1977.

St. Clair, Raquel Annette, and William D. Watley. *The African Presence in the Bible: Gospel Sermons Rooted in History.* Valley Forge, Pa.: Judson Press, 2000

Selected Womanist Major Works

Cannon, Katie G. *Black Womanist Ethics.* Atlanta: Scholars Press, 1988.

____. *Katie's Canon: Womanism and the Soul of the Black Community.* New York: Continuum, 1995.

____. *Teaching Preaching: Isaac Rufus Clark and Black Sacred Rhetoric.* New York: Continuum, 2002.

____, and Carter Heyward. *Alienation and Anger: A Black and a White Woman's Struggle for Mutuality in an Unjust World.* Wellesley, Mass.: The Stone Center, 1992.

____, and the Mud Flower Collective. *God's Fierce Whimsy: Christian Feminism and Theological Education.* New York: Pilgrim Press, 1985.

Copeland, M. Shawn, and Elisabeth Schüssler Fiorenza, eds. *Feminist Theology in Different Contexts.* London: SCM Press; Maryknoll, N.Y.: Orbis Books, 1996.

____. *Violence Against Women.* London: SCM Press; Maryknoll, N.Y.: Orbis Books, 1994.

Fry Brown, Teresa. "An African American Woman's Perspective: Renovating Sorrow's Kitchen" In *Preaching Justice: Ethnic and Cultural Perspectives,* edited by Christine M. Smith. Cleveland: United Church Press, 1998.

____. *God Don't Like Ugly: African American Women Handing on Spiritual Values.* Nashville: Abingdon Press, 2000.

Gilkes, Cheryl Townsend. *"If It Wasn't For the Women…": Black Women's Experience and Womanist Culture in Church and Community.* Maryknoll, N.Y.: Orbis Books, 2001.

Grant, Jacquelyn. *White Women's Christ, Black Women's Jesus: Feminist Christology and Womanist Response.* Atlanta: Scholars Press, 1989.

_____, ed. *Perspectives on Womanist Theology*. Black Church Scholars. Atlanta: The ITC Press, 1995.

_____, and Randall C. Bailey, eds. *The Recovery of Black Presence: An Interdisciplinary Exploration: Essays in Honor of D. Charles B. Copher*. Nashville: Abingdon Press, 1995.

McKenzie, Vashti M. *Not Without a Struggle: Leadership Development for African American Women in Ministry*. Cleveland: United Church Press, 1996.

_____. *Strength in the Struggle: Leadership Development for Women*. Cleveland: Pilgrim Press, 1997.

Riggs, Marcia Y. *Awake, Arise, & Act: A Womanist Call for Black Liberation*. Cleveland: Pilgrim Press, 1994.

_____. *The Kelly Miller Smith Papers*. Arranged and described by Marcia Riggs. Nashville: Jean and Alexander Heard Library at Vanderbilt University, 1989.

_____. *Toward a Mediating Ethic for Black Liberation: Ethical Insights of Black Female Reformers of the Nineteenth Century*. Ph.D. diss., Vanderbilt University, 1991.

_____, ed. *Can I Get a Witness?: Prophetic Religious Voices of African American Women: An Anthology*. Maryknoll, N.Y.: Orbis Books, 1997.

Sanders, Cheryl Jean. *Empowerment Ethics for a Liberated People: A Path to African American Social Transformation*. Minneapolis: Fortress Press, 1995.

_____. *Living the Intersection: Womanism and Afrocentrism in Theology*. Minneapolis: Fortress Press, 1995.

_____. *Ministry at the Margins: The Prophetic Mission of Women, Youth & The Poor*. Downers Grove, Ill.: InterVarsity Press, 1997.

_____. *Saints in Exile: The Holiness-Pentecostal Experience in African American Religion and Culture*. New York: Oxford University Press, 1996.

Townes, Emilie M. *Breaking the Fine Rain of Death: African American Health Issues and a Womanist Ethic of Care*. New York: Continuum, 1998.

_____. *In a Blaze of Glory: Womanist Spirituality as Social Witness*. Nashville: Abingdon Press, 1995.

_____. *The Kingdom of God in Black Preaching: An Analysis and Critique of James H. Cone*. D.Min. thesis, University of Chicago, Divinity School, 1982.

_____. *Womanist Justice, Womanist Hope*. Atlanta: Scholars Press, 1993.

_____, ed. *A Troubling in My Soul: Womanist Perspectives on Evil and Suffering*. Maryknoll, N.Y.: Orbis Books, 1993.

_____, ed. *Embracing the Spirit: Womanist Perspectives on Hope, Salvation, and Transformation*. Maryknoll, N.Y.: Orbis Books, 1997.

Weems, Renita J. *Battered Love: Marriage, Sex, and Violence in the Hebrew Prophets*. Minneapolis: Fortress Press, 1995.

_____. *I Asked for Intimacy: Stories of Blessings, Betrayals, and Birthings*. San Diego: LuraMedia, 1993.

_____. *Just a Sister Away: A Womanist Vision of Women's Relationships in the Bible*. San Diego: LuraMedia, 1988.

_____. *Listening for God: A Minister's Journey through Silence and Doubt*. New York: Simon & Schuster, 1999.

Williams, Delores S. *Black Theology in a New Key: Feminist Theology in a Different Voice*. Maryknoll, N.Y.: Orbis Books, 1996.

_____. *Sisters in the Wilderness: The Challenge of Womanist God-Talk*. Maryknoll, N.Y.: Orbis Books, 1993.